W9-BRC-066

CELEBRITIES ON THE COUCH

Other Books by Lucy Freeman

Fight Against Fears
Before I Kill More
So You Want to be Psychoanalyzed
The Cry for Love
Farewell to Fear

CELEBRITIES ON THE COUCH

Personal Adventures of Famous People in Psychoanalysis

**Edited by
Lucy Freeman**

PRICE/STERN/SLOAN
Publishers, Inc.
and
RAVENNA BOOKS
Los Angeles

Copyright © by Lucy Freeman
Published by Price/Stern/Sloan Publishers, Inc. — Ravenna Books, Inc.
Printed in the United States of America. All Rights Reserved
410 North La Cienega Boulevard, Los Angeles, California 90048
Library of Congress Catalog Card Number: 67-16399

Permissions — Celebrities On The Couch

The following permissions are gratefully acknowledged:

Patty Duke. Excerpt from *Back From 'Valley of the Dolls'* by Rex Reed © 1969 by The New York Times, reprinted with the permission of Rex Reed and The New York Times.

Tennessee Williams. Opening Some Doors by Don Ross, reprinted with the permission of the Herald Tribune, New York.

Excerpt from *The Lost Childhood And Other Essays* by Graham Greene, copyright © 1951 by Graham Greene, reprinted with the permission of Eyre and Spottiswoode, Ltd., London, and The Viking Press, Inc., New York.

Josh Logan, copyright © 1949 by Time, Inc. From the book *Writing on Life: Sixteen Closeups,* copyright © 1951 by Lincoln Barnett, reprinted by permission of William Morrow and Company, New York.

What Psychoanalysis Did for Me by Sid Caesar, As Told To Richard Gehman, reprinted with the permission of Richard Gehman.

The Alien Voice Within by Hermann Hesse, published by The Psychoanalytic Review, Vol. 50, No. 3, Fall of 1963, reprinted with the permission of The Psychoanalytic Review. Originally published as H. Hesse, Kunstler und Psychoanalyse. Almanach fur das Jahr 1926. Vienna: Internationaler Psychoanalytischer Verlag, 1926. I, 34-38.

contents

SID CAESAR
What Psychoanalysis Did For Me 27

"I was a success. I had a lovely and devoted wife, a darling little girl. The future looked bright. I was miserable."

JAYNE MEADOWS
The Two Jaynes 41

"Steve Allen was everything that appealed to me in a man. But our marriage couldn't have worked if I hadn't had psychiatric help."

TENNESSEE WILLIAMS
Opening Some Doors by Don Ross 53

"He hit me where it hurts most. He said I wrote cheap melodrama."

acknowledgments

Deepest thanks to Irving Wallace, who conceived the idea of this book and its provocative title; to Auriel Douglas and Cynthia White for their editorial help in shaping the book; to Herbert Alexander, who suggested me as editor; to L. L. Sloan, publisher with faith; to Liselotte Bendix, librarian at the New York Psychoanalytic Institute; to Madeleine Paley, who helped on a chapter; to Floyd Patterson, who graciously consented to give an interview, and to all the others who are part of this book.

CELEBRITIES ON THE COUCH

Good-Bye "Anna O,"
Hello Sid Caesar

In 1605, a man who understood the human heart, William Shakespeare, wrote in *MacBeth:*

> Canst thou not minister to a mind diseas'd
> Pluck from the memory a rooted sorrow,
> Raze out the written troubles of the brain,
> And with some sweet oblivious antidote
> Cleanse the stuff'd bosom of that perilous stuff
> Which weighs about the heart?

Canst thou not minister to a mind . . . ?

Before the turn of this century, Dr. Sigmund Freud had answered Shakespeare in the affirmative. As have thousands of psychoanalysts who followed in Freud's footsteps.

Today, psychoanalysis and other forms of therapy are almost universally accepted by the medical profession and a large part of the public as a useful and successful means of ministering to a mind.

Not so long ago, when the general public was still quite ignorant about the subject, many who had undergone psychoanalysis and who benefited from it, either were ashamed or afraid to admit it. Those in the public eye or well-known in their professions, who depended on the respect of the public or colleagues, were loathe to speak of having been "on the couch" or having received psychic "help" in any form. It is reported that when a wealthy woman friend offered to finance psychoanalytic treatment for novelist James Joyce in Switzerland, Joyce refused, horrified.

Today, with greater acceptance of psychoanalysis by the public, this attitude has changed. Many famous persons in various fields, who have undergone successful therapy, are willing, sometimes eager, to speak of their treatment publicly, because they wish to help others. In the 1930s, Moss Hart, who up until then had only collaborated on plays, went into an analysis about which he spoke freely. One of his biographers, Margaret Case Harriman, wrote, "Now in his sixth year of psychiatry, Hart says he thinks he can see the end. His friends declare that he is a new man, and no one can deny that psychiatry, or something, has enabled him to write three plays alone, independent of any collaborator."

Today, hardly a week passes that we do not read in the press, or hear personally, that some celebrity has told of his analysis and spoken with praise of the results. In the entertainment world, Sid Caesar, Josh Logan, Patty Duke, Vivian Vance, to cite a few, have expressed themselves freely on the printed page as to how their lives have been improved by psychological help. Recently, actor Rod Steiger stated, "One of the things which analysis did for me was to enable me to substitute one set of problems for another, but the second set was easier to cope with." Another actor, Ben Gazzara, had no reservations when he summed up his therapy by saying, "Thanks to analysis I've adjusted now and have perspective about myself and my craft." The young film star, Natalie Wood, told the *New York Times,* "It was the most valuable help of any single thing in my life. Because of it, I've been able to make the kind of changes within myself I've wanted."

The internationally known actor, Marlon Brando, confessed, "The principal benefit acting has afforded me is the money to pay my psychiatrist."

In another field entirely, that of religion, the Reverend Harry B. Scholefield, D.D., Minister of the First Unitarian Church of San Francisco, commented: "The positive effect that the analysis had on me in the area of preaching may be summed up as follows. In arriving at a higher degree of self-acceptance and self-knowledge, I resolved, or at least began to see, some of the conflicts underlying the excessive difficulty I experienced in sermon preparation. I became aware that many of the uses I was making of sermons or sermonizing were at variance with my conscious intent. I lived through a good many conflicts. I had a good many encounters with my unconscious, which at first I denied were relevant to the problems inherent in sermon composition. But as I lived through these encounters, I began to see that I did have a right to preach, and I began gradually to put a fresh and higher value on the pulpit and its varied meanings."

This book was prepared by personal interviews, correspondence and telephone conversations with numerous celebrities. Some who had been in analysis did not wish to speak at length about it but did not object to being quoted briefly. Playwright Abe Burrows said, "I found analysis wonderful—but I don't want to talk about it." Actor Tony Randall practically echoed these words, saying, "I won't tell you why I went into treatment, but I certainly got a lot out of it." Margie Hart, the stripteaser, said, "Thanks to psychoanalysis, I don't hate Margie Hart anymore."

Others were willing to be quoted at length, feeling that the climate of the times made it possible for them to speak of their treatment. Thus this unique book was made possible.

For the first time, it is believed, a group of renowned persons have been brought together in one volume to describe to readers details of the personal problems that sent them into analysis and of the progress and results of their individual experience on the analyst's couch or in other types of psychic treatment.

There have been previous collections of case histories written by psychoanalysts. But, because of the ethics of the medical profession, the identity of the patients in most of these cases has been hidden behind numerals or letters or pseudonyms, such as Case 29 or Case B or Miss Henrietta.

But now, celebrities who have benefited from therapy have agreed to stand up and be counted—by name. And in these pages, they have recounted courageously, with candor, how they found their personal truths and gained emotional strength at last.

The readiness of these celebrities to speak out honestly in print is, in a sense, a milestone in the acceptance of a therapeutic process that started in Vienna in 1893, upon publication of a case history by Freud and Josef Breuer about a woman to whom they gave the pseudonym, Anna O. A patient of Breuer's, she was identified years later as Bertha Pappenheim, a wealthy, beautiful young woman whom Breuer cured of many symptoms of emotional distress.

Now, it is Good-Bye, "Anna O."

Now, it is Sid Caesar, not "Mr. O." Josh Logan, not "J. O." Vivian Vance, not "Mary O."

While the title of the book is *Celebrities on the Couch,* strictly speaking it is concerned not only with the couch but also the chair, and not only with psychoanalysis but other forms of therapy as well. In psychoanalysis the couch is the place on which the patient takes his inner journey to freedom. The chair is used, as a rule, for all other forms of psychological treatment.

Although most of the contributors are known coast-to-coast, even internationally, some are prominent chiefly in their particular profession. Some may not be as well-known to readers as others, but they have important things to say about their lives before, during, or after treatment.

Although the entire book could have been written by celebrities in Hollywood, on Broadway, or in television, it includes not only actors and actresses but celebrities from the world of sports, jazz, photography, advertising, literature, public relations and psychoanalysis itself—one psychoanalyst writes of his analysis with Ferenczi, one of Freud's first students and closest friends.

Each contributor has a different story to tell, since every analysis is different. Some have drawn a general picture of their experience. Others emphasize only one aspect. Still others have presented several facets of their journey into the unconscious.

A few have been critical of analysis, feeling they should have gotten more out of it.

The contributors went into analysis for a variety of reasons: a baseball player was unable to control his temper with managers, umpires and his fellow players; an advertising executive sought help for one of his colleagues and was advised to seek it for himself; a publicist suffered digestive ailments; a psychoanalyst needed it as part of his training.

Some contributors look back on their experience over a distance of fifteen or twenty years. Some have recently finished treatment. Others are just starting.

It is hoped the book will bring even more acceptance to the art-science that has so recently come into being and new hope to those who suffer because of emotional conflicts and are willing to invest time, money and effort to make their lives happier.

Lucy Freeman

What Psychoanalysis Did for Me
By Sid Caesar
as told to Richard Gehman

---

*Famed comedian, Sid Caesar is perhaps best known as Imo-
gene Coca's partner in the highly successful television comedy
hour of some years ago, "Your Show of Shows." He also starred
for several seasons on his own show, "Caesar's Hour." Mr.
Caesar played the leading role in the Broadway hit* Little Me
*and has performed with equal brilliance in nightclubs across
the country.*

I have agreed to do this article because I want to use myself
as an example. It's a miracle that I didn't wind up as a juvenile
delinquent. I know this because the science of psychoanalysis
has helped me to evaluate my own experiences, many of which
were no different from those which have made delinquents out
of thousands of other children.

For example, when I was about five, my parents had a disagreement which resulted in my mother leaving our home in Yonkers, New York, and going off to stay with friends in Asbury Park, New Jersey, for a few days. My father was trying to make a go of the restaurant he owned and was too busy to look after me. Finally, he put a card that said "Asbury Park" around my neck and packed me off on a train, asking a conductor to keep an eye on me. I was terrified. I kept watching the conductor, afraid he would forget about me, but I was too timid and embarrassed to ask him when we would get there. As the train pulled into Asbury Park, it was raining hard. The conductor put me off—just in time for me to see another train pulling out in the opposite direction, and my mother sitting by one of the windows.

My father had not bothered to call her. I stood there, lost and hopeless, until the people who had brought my mother to the station happened to catch sight of me. They took me to their house. "Don't worry," they said, "we'll see that you get back home." But later that day, I was in for another disappointment when they called my parents. They asked them to keep me for a couple of days. If my mother and father had beaten me with baseball bats, they couldn't have hurt me half as much.

The wound that incident left in me was further infected by other bad experiences which ultimately gained control of my life and influenced my entire personality. When a man steps on a nail, he cannot walk without favoring his sore foot. Unless he gets rid of the nail, the wound will become infected and he will go through life with a limp. The pain may become so great that most of his time will be taken up with worry over his foot, and he will have no time for the normal pursuit of happiness, which is every person's right. So it is with emotional wounds—which we call neuroses.

By the time I was twenty-seven, I had such a collection of emotional scars I spent most of my time worrying about them, and the rest of it feeling sorry for myself. That was in 1950, the year I was enjoying my first success in television on NBC's "Your Show of Shows." Except that I wasn't enjoying it. A year or two before, I had been wondering where my next buck was coming from. Now, practically overnight, I was a success, earning $2,250 a week and well on my way to financial security. I had a lovely and devoted wife, a darling little girl, and a pleasant home. The future looked bright. And still I was miserable.

For reasons I didn't know, it seemed impossible for me to be happy. Even when one of my shows came off especially well, I would walk out of the studio with a feeling of deep depression. Stupid though it may sound, I felt as though I was having too much luck—and that if I acted as though I enjoyed it, the luck would leave. Therefore, if I behaved as though I was unlucky, and remained depressed, melancholy, and miserable, I would always be lucky.

On stage, I could hide behind the characters and inanimate objects I created. Off stage, with my real personality bared for all to see, I was a mess. It was difficult for me to establish a normal, healthy relationship with anyone. I couldn't believe that anyone could like me for myself. I thought people went around with me because they wanted something from me.

My life was full of small irritations. The telephone, for instance—I hated to talk on it. The person on the other end always sounded so cold and removed, I would somehow get the idea he was hostile. Even my wife sounded that way. "Why do you sound so cold?" I'd demand. "What's bothering you?" "Nothing," she would say. "What's bothering you?" "Nothing," I would shout, "but I know something's bothering you."

I was continually causing contention in our house; I bickered whenever my wife and I were together. I don't know how she stood me.

Looking back, there were some good surface reasons for my uneasiness. I knew I was lucky to have gotten into TV on the ground floor, and I had no faith in my ability to keep it up. If my head writer, Mel Tolkin, said, "Wonderful show, Sid," I would cringe.

"Don't say that too loud," I would say. "Luck might hear you. Besides, what about next week? Can I do it again?"

That question hounded me even when I tried to sleep. I had less than the normal amount of self-confidence—so much less that the only thing I was confident of was that I had no confidence whatever. Later, when in psychoanalysis I finally had the courage to face my inner self, I was reminded of the time when I was a boy and took up weight lifting. In school, I hated to fight. What did I do? I developed tremendous muscles which everyone had to respect. The biceps I built were nothing but disguises for my fear. I now realize that I spent much of my life building disguises and defenses. At twenty-seven, I was so emotionally muscle-bound I could scarcely move.

Then, one day I went to a physician for a complete checkup. I thought there was something wrong with me. After examining me from head to toe, he said, "There's nothing physically wrong at all."

I felt fine until I got out of his office. *What had he meant by that? Had he meant . . . no, that was impossible. I work, I told myself, I get along with people, and there's nothing about myself I don't know, since I spend so much time thinking and worrying about myself. Go to a psychiatrist? I wouldn't have the time. And what if people found out? Besides, I don't need one. I'm all right. I feel great.*

Despite the great strides we've made in the twentieth century in knowledge and understanding and communication, many of us still tend to think of psychoanalysis as something similar to magic. That was how I felt. I did not realize then that the doctor is only a teacher and guide in a prolonged, arduous struggle for self-understanding. So, when I approached his office, I was half-expecting a man with a spade beard and piercing eyes: a magician.

Instead, I found a personable, soft-spoken fellow of about forty-four, very polite and with a pleasing manner. Dr. X, as I will call him here, had undergone an extended period of preparation for his lifework. The science of helping people attain happiness cannot be mastered overnight. To become a fully qualified analyst, a man must be an M.D. He must be psychoanalyzed himself, which takes anywhere from two to five years, or longer. He must spend a minimum of one year in general hospital internship and three years as a resident psychiatrist in hospitals or clinics. Only then may he practice.

Although Dr. X's appearance was disarming enough, I was rather upset by his frankness. After gathering the usual facts about my physical history and family background, he began asking intimate questions about my life. "What business is that of yours?" I asked.

"If you won't answer," he said, "there's no way I can help you."

So I began to tell him what I could, little realizing that I actually did not know much about myself, principally because I would not let myself know. Like many disturbed people, my problems were caused in a large part by a profound feeling of inadequacy which had a basis in my childhood. To borrow a phrase from the Bible and paraphrase it, I was a man, but I thought and behaved like a child. I could not accept my manhood because somewhere I wanted to remain a passive, dependent child.

After that first hour, I felt naked. I was not sure I wanted to go on. I could not see the value of prying into those areas of my mind that were better left unexplored. The fact is, I was scared silly. But I knew that something had to be done. Like the man with the nail in his foot, I was in real pain—and although the pain increased every time the analyst touched a sensitive spot, I knew the wound had to be probed if I was to make progress.

So began the most trying period of my life. I had to go to Dr. X's office and lie on a couch for one hour each day, five days a week—an analyst's hour, which is only 50 minutes long. In itself, that was a degrading experience—or so it seemed. I was baring my innermost soul, attempting to let the truth come out as I saw it, saying anything that came into my head in free association so that he could get some clues to what was bothering me. I felt low in the doctor's presence because I had a low opinion of myself. I thought, *How can he take an interest in me?* After the shameful things I thought I'd done, I didn't see how he could have any regard for me.

That attitude, I now realize, was another defense I was set-
ting up to keep myself from getting at the truth. Also, I felt a
real hostility toward the doctor, because he was taking so much
of my money. What I did not know was that I was angry at myself because I would not tell him the truth. It was I who was
wasting money—because I was reluctant to explore the things
that were bothering me.

Before long, I learned the meanings of the words "conscious" and "unconscious" as the psychoanalyst uses them. My
unconscious, I found out, was the storehouse of my brain—it
took in everything I'd seen, heard, felt, tasted, and smelled,
and stored it away. The conscious—that part which made the
personality I showed to the rest of the world—acted as a guard
for the storehouse. It would not let me recall completely what
I'd seen, heard, felt, tasted, and smelled. It was a censor, too,
who would let out only what I wanted others to see and held
back what I didn't want them to know about. Put it this way: I
learned that the conscious was the personality I was, and the
unconscious was the personality I was trying not to be.

At the time I first went into treatment, I was walking around
with a collection of personal superstitions. I never would get
a haircut. My wife would have to prod me for weeks before I'd
go to a barber. With Dr. X's help, I found out the reason—it
was because of a boyish superstition buried in my unconscious.
It involved the story of Samson losing his strength when he lost
his hair. Without my knowing it, that story had made a real
impression on me. All kids have superstitions they pick up
without knowing their importance. I was fortunate. Mine only
made me look shaggy and ridiculous.

I began trying to trace other superstitions and false concepts.

I revisited my childhood every day, looking for incidents that had affected me. Early in the process, I told the doctor about my pervading feeling of guilt, which overshadowed everything I did. I recalled a time in grade school when someone had stolen another kid's fountain pen. The teacher said, "We will file into the cloakroom, and the person who stole the pen will leave it there."

I hadn't stolen that pen, but something in the teacher's manner made me think she was speaking directly to me. I *felt* as if I had stolen it, and what was worse, I thought everybody else thought I had. It seemed they were all accusing me.

Another episode I recalled happened when I was about four. We lived a few doors from a laundry. Everybody else in our family worked in my father's restaurant, and I was left to myself most of the time. One way I liked to pass time was to go to the laundry and watch the guys load trucks. One day while I was standing there, one of them came over with the nozzle of a hose in his hand.

"Want to take this home, sonny?" he asked. He was holding it so that I didn't see it was connected. "Go ahead, take it home," he said. As I started to walk away, he turned on the water. I was soaked to the skin, and I went nearly blind with fear and anger.

These and other instances, magnified and reenacted millions of times in my mind, grew all out of proportion to their importance. I could never stand any situation in which I was not in complete control. As I grew older, this fear developed new dimensions. If I was driving a car and did not know how to get where I was going, I wouldn't go. I would refuse to drive— afraid I'd make a fool of myself in not knowing how to get there directly.

My mother and father were immigrants. He was from Austrian Poland and she was from Odessa. They came to this country as children, and their lives consisted of nothing but hard work. I was born September 8, 1922—the fourth child. I had three older brothers, but I came along ten years after my parents' third son was born. So, from as far back as I could recall, I was a midget in a world of monsters—and, not only that, giants who did not want me. Or so I thought. Although most children did not start school until the age of six, they sent me when I was four—just to get me out of the house.

I never had the feeling of being wanted by my family and, as a result, I would constantly go in search of attention. One day, I told my analyst, two of my uncles and their wives came to visit. They gave me a big "hello," remarked on how big I'd grown, and then the men began to play pinochle and the women to gossip. I was determined to make them notice me. It was raining outside. I thought, *I'll go out, get wet, catch a cold and die, and then they'll all be sorry.* What happened was that my parents punished me and put me to bed. But even that was gratifying, for at least I got some attention.

I don't mean to say that, as my analysis progressed, I came to believe that everything that was the matter with me was the fault of my parents. Far from it. I came to learn that they had caused part of my trouble, because they were troubled. Once I grasped that, I lost some of the resentment I'd had for them—the hatred which ultimately turned inward. And I also learned that any child is molded by the sum of his experiences in and out of the home. One of the most important factors is his choice of heroes. If he is fortunate enough to run around with an athletic crowd, his heroes will most likely be athletes. But suppose his hero is the bully from the next block, who thinks it's a great deed of bravery to peg a rock through a window. This boy is bound to get into trouble. I was lucky. Someone left an old saxophone in my father's restaurant. With his encouragement, I started to play it and found I liked it—and my first idol was Benny Goodman. I've often been glad that no one ever left a sawed-off shotgun.

These and other experiences, all significant, all meaningful when related to the pattern of my life, came out one by one as I lay day by day on that doctor's couch. They did not come easily. The unconscious is jealous of its secrets. It takes great pleasure in its fears and terrors. But it cannot keep from revealing itself in dreams. Whenever I dreamed, I would tell the doctor, and he and I would try to unravel the dream's meaning.

Like most people in treatment, I went through several stages. In the first, I experienced a feeling of skepticism and complete mistrust. The analyst was my enemy—and an expensive enemy, too. *If he's so interested in my case,* I reasoned, *why is he taking my money?*

During the second stage, my resentment changed to a childish attempt at friendliness. I loved him and tried to win his approval—so he would not make me tell him the "dark secrets" I was hiding. Once, I bought a watch and presented it to him. "Don't you know you are trying to bribe me?" he said. "I can't accept this watch." It was as if he were saying, *But don't worry, Sid, I won't tell anybody what a bad boy you think you've been.* Gradually, I came to realize that these gestures of friendship actually hid my resentment.

In the third stage, I was convinced that I knew more than the analyst did. I constantly theorized, drawing conclusions which were very "scientific" but which had nothing to do with my case.

In the fourth stage, I knew so much that I was sure I was beyond assistance. "This man can do nothing for me," I said flatly to my wife, thereby violating his rule that I must not discuss treatment outside the office. "It's nothing but a waste of time and money." There had been days when the sun broke through and I left the doctor's office floating with new knowledge and inner security. But they were always followed immediately by the overcast gloom that had been the pattern of my pre-analysis life.

Then I understood that these stages were all parts of my resistance—for analysis, after all, is nothing more than the gradual breaking down of a person's resistance to the unlocking of his unconscious.

Oddly enough, the fourth stage modulated into the fifth. It gradually dawned on me that I had to stop theorizing and get down to reality. I had to realize that the analyst was just another man with great understanding and, above all, great patience, who was assisting me to understand my wounds of childhood and to realize that they no longer mattered. Now, the pampering period was over, and the time had come for me to put into practice all the theories I'd learned if I was ever going to be a happy person.

Today, I think of my analysis in this way: There's a desk sitting in a dark room. I open the door, rush in, and hit the desk. I hurt myself. Why? I didn't see it. I rush back a little distance, saying, *I'm going to get there*. Clunk! It happens again and again. Then someone—the doctor—says, *Hey, why don't you put on the light?*

That's what psychoanalysis is. It will not take away the desk, but it enables a man to walk around it. Many people make the mistake of believing that this process happens at once, or that they can find short cuts. A few hours of therapy may assist some people—a talk with a clergyman, a psychiatrist, or a psychologist may help one get through or avoid a pressing problem. But while that may provide some temporary help, the neurosis frequently remains until it is sought out and traced to its source by hard, unrelenting, and unending work that real analysis must necessarily involve.

What did my analysis do for me in concrete terms? First, it made me aware of the eruptions and upheavals of anger and resentment, murderous drives developed in childhood, which had no outlet—the very feelings which could have turned me into a delinquent. In one sense, I was a delinquent; I had to take those feelings out on someone. I took them out on the nearest person to me—myself. I wouldn't let myself be happy for any money.

Once I made clear to myself that those childhood incidents were in the past, I found I could start a new life. In short, I found I was no longer a child but a grown man, and because I was grown, no problem could loom as large as it had in the days when I was surrounded by giants.

Then, too, my work began to improve [on " Caesar's Hour" (NBC-TV)—Ed.] It formerly took me an entire day to accomplish what I now can get done in a few hours, simply because I no longer waste so much time worrying over and cherishing my neuroses. And it has helped me because I now believe I have a deeper feeling for the idiosyncrasies and foibles on which so much humor is predicated. It used to be that a good deal of my comedy made sport of people. In a sense, it was another outlet for my inner anger, for satire is angry humor. Now, I try to use myself as a mirror in which others can see their behavior.

I am less irritable at home. I have come to regard my wife not only as someone I'm married to, but as my dear friend, someone who understands me and someone on whom I can lean when I have to.

To sum it all up, I found that, by developing self-respect, you will inevitably learn to respect others.

To most people, these things may sound like nothing but good common sense. To me, to understand them was a great achievement. It is an achievement that is being duplicated in psychoanalytic treatment by many people who otherwise might be deeply troubled. In the years to come, many others will be getting the same benefits, for we are growing more and more conscious of this science.

This brings me to the most important thing I learned in analysis. I said before that there are no short cuts, but there is one thing that parents can apply to keep their children from becoming delinquents and to keep the disturbed ones from going through the long, arduous, and expensive treatment I had to undergo.

It's called love.

The Two Jaynes
By Jayne Meadows

Broadway actress, film star and television personality, Miss Meadows in private life is Mrs. Steve Allen.

I went into analysis for the very simple reason that I was unhappy with myself and with everything around me.

But then, I had been unhappy for many years. Not constantly, of course, but the teenage years had been particularly painful for me. I was frightened and insecure as well as poor. Unsure of myself, I doubted my physical attractiveness. There were times when I did feel more attractive than others. But most of the time I thought I was decidedly below average.

I was hounded by mysterious allergies and had, in fact, been labeled by several doctors one of the worst cases of allergy they had ever seen. But these allergies took strange forms. Sometimes I would suffer from a particular allergy. At other times I would be free of it.

I needed love and approval desperately and yet was very fickle and infantile in my love relationships. I had many boyfriends, but none of my relationships were deep because I wouldn't allow it.

I didn't escape into the world of alcohol or of dope addiction perhaps because of my background. As the daughter of Protestant missionaries, raised in the bosom of the church, I had been brought up in a home where no one smoked and liquor was never served. Instead, I escaped into the highly neurotic world of show-business where I hoped to become famous and loved by everybody.

As it happened, I was successful in my career right from the start. Only a few months out of high school, I was playing ingenue leads on Broadway, in one successful play after another, and I was never out of work for more than a few weeks at a time.

I now realize that it was fortunate for me that my world collapsed all at once and at a very early age. I fell in love unrequitedly at the same time that I ran into an impasse in my career. I was cast in the leading role of a Broadway play. My role was both unbelievable and unplayable. Every young actress on Broadway had read for the part, but I was unlucky enough to get it. In spite of the fact that the play was a hit and ran for four to five months, I regressed more and more emotionally during this period.

As a child I had been open, gregarious, highstrung, optimistic, and always ready for a party. Now I went nowhere, saw no one except when my work called for it. I suffered from allergy, cramps, pains in the shoulders, all kinds of imaginary illnesses, and I spent hours alone in my apartment just crying.

During this period I started to study acting for the first time, even though I had already played leads in five or six Broadway shows. It was my drama teacher who first mentioned the possibility that I might benefit from psychoanalysis. He noticed that I shied away from playing emotional roles. When he tried to trick me through improvisations, assigning me a tragic situation, I always managed to squirm out by turning it into comedy.

When he first mentioned the subject of psychiatry to me, I responded with alarm since in the almost Victorian social climate of my childhood a *psychiatrist* was practically synonymous with an abortionist. No one that I knew or had grown up with had ever been to a psychiatrist, or even met one, as far as I remember. One of my friends had committed suicide and several had been confined to mental institutions, but that was something no one ever talked about. It was about this time that I learned that my maternal grandmother had died in a mental institution where she had resided for many years.

I cannot recall now from whom I got the name of the first psychiatrist whom I interviewed, but I do remember vividly my appointment with him. I have completely blocked out his name and address, but I recall that it was a beautiful spring afternoon in New York when I walked to his office, somewhere in mid-Manhattan. I was, in fact, in a very good mood as I approached the appointment because I had such a longing for help.

But his waiting room made me uncomfortable. The only thing I remember about it now is that there was a large glass cabinet full of medical instruments. And the doctor himself scared me to death. He was a tall, muscular German with a heavy accent and a bald head, somewhere in his middle years. His manner was not at all unpleasant, but the combination of the guttural accent and his scientific questioning on age, profession, and so forth put me on the defensive, and his question, "Have you ever been bothered by stage-fright?" caused me such panic that I became claustrophobic and couldn't wait to escape.

I confided this shattering experience to my drama coach who went immediately to the phone and made an appointment for me to visit a psychologist he knew on the following day. The simple presence of this sweet, kindly woman with her soft Viennese accent so relaxed me emotionally that I was able to reveal things to her that I had never told anyone else in the world. She arranged for me to take a Rorschach test the following Sunday—my only day off from the play. The test took only three hours, but I was so completely drained emotionally, so physically exhausted as a result of it that I asked to sit a little while before trying to go home. I was as weak as any patient coming out of ether after a serious operation.

Sometime later when I was able to read the results of the test, I remembered that in one of the blots I had seen what looked to me like a deer and when asked by the psychologist what the deer was doing, I said, "It's flying through the sky." To which she responded, "Oh, do deer ever fly through the sky?"

"Of course," I replied. "Santa Claus's reindeer do."

And that was the theme of my whole Rorschach test, one of infantile imagery, fantasy, and fairytales. It was interesting that the Rorschach test revealed that my native ability seemed to lie in the field of acting and it was even suggested that acting might be a good form of therapy for me.

I only had about ten sessions with this psychologist when my career took me to Hollywood where I had signed a contract with Metro-Goldwyn-Mayer Studios. At this point an interesting thing happened.

The powers-that-be at MGM, after seeing my screen test, decided that my real quality was that of a young Margaret Sullavan or Ingrid Bergman. They proceeded to cast me in a series of extremely dramatic character parts which were so well-received by the critics that I began getting more and more dramatic roles. Because I now work mostly in comedy, it's a constant source of amusement, or I should say amazement, to my television fans when they see me on the late-late show in one of these serious dramatic parts.

At the time, lacking any sense of reality, I began to identify with a number of these roles and to become depressed by them. Since troubles never come singly to a neurotic, I repeated my unhealthy romantic pattern by falling in love with and marrying a man old enough to be my father. I did not enjoy my career, I did not feel free with my associates, and once more the walls of life began to close in on me.

But this time I went in search of help. I found a doctor in Los Angeles. This brilliant and sensitive psychiatrist gave me the courage and strength to break the unusually strong, neurotic ties with my family and to see that it was possible for me to really love my parents in a healthy way. For the first time I was able to see them as human beings with human weaknesses and not as the all-powerful authority figures which had so frightened me in the past.

My work with the doctor made it possible for me to see myself as a woman who might settle down with one man. While my marriage to a man more than twice my age was doomed to failure, I was able to handle the break-up with a minimum of guilt. I picked up the pieces, moved back to New York City and the stage, leaving behind the lucrative movie fields. While I had been toiling on the sound-stages of Hollywood, television had become a thriving industry in New York. Younger, faster, and infinitely more demanding than either the stage or the movies, the new medium petrified me.

Those were the days of the live shows shot without the benefit of long hours of rehearsals which one has on Broadway and without the possibility of retakes by which a performer in Hollywood is protected. The four years of daily visits to the psychiatrist in Los Angeles had not been enough to resolve all my problems, So I returned to the woman who had originally helped me in New York. She suggested that it might be a good idea to take a Rorschach test again, since five years had passed. This time the hours passed like minutes and I was in a happy frame of mind when I finished. In fact I tried to find the card where I had originally seen Santa Claus's reindeer, but I couldn't find them. All the terror, all the anxiety that I had felt during the first test was gone. Nevertheless, I needed to continue my analysis to cope not only with a new medium and all its pressures, but with my new life.

I was still playing highly emotional roles. One of my first parts in television was on the old "Robert Montgomery Presents" show, in which I played twin sisters, one good and one evil. Part of the format of this program was to bring the stars out at the end of the story to take a bow and to chat for a few minutes with Robert Montgomery.

My psychologist watched the program, and the next day in our session she remarked on the difference between the two Jaynes, the one who played the role and the "radiant" Jayne who appeared as herself at the end of the program. This was a word that had frequently been used to describe me in childhood, but it had ceased to apply to me for many, many years.

Six months later I auditioned for a new panel show called "I've Got A Secret." The program had been on the air for several weeks but had not been very well-received by the critics. When Mark Goodson, the producer, engaged me for the show, he said, "I like your personality, I think it's very commercial. I don't know what it is, I think it's a saucy quality, but I think I can capitalize on it." After several weeks CBS made a test to determine audience reaction to me. The consensus of the audience was that I had a "radiant" personality, and I was signed to a long-term contract.

A year ago I played a role in a television series at MGM, and as a result of this performance was asked to make a pilot for a new series which was to be shot during the Christmas holidays. The script was excellent, but I bowed out saying that unfortunately the children were home from school during the Christmas season and that I was very busy shopping and wrapping presents and so was unable to find the time to make the pilot. Finally, after all other channels had failed, the head of television production prevailed on me, saying, "We need you very much for this role, and if you don't do it you will never work again at MGM."

I laughed and said, "Oh, that's ridiculous. I can suggest any number of actresses who could play this part."

But when I gave him their names, all well-established stars, he said, "But they do not have your quality. We need your radiance and your gaiety in this role."

I thanked him and declined, but when I put up the phone I laughed. I could never have believed, ten years before, that anyone would be saying to me, "No one in the business has this certain quality but you."

I remained in analysis during the seven years I worked on "I've Got A Secret." At first I had daily sessions. Towards the end they were cut to weekly appointments.

The first night I appeared on "I've Got A Secret" I met the man who was to become my husband, Steve Allen. My sister Audrey had invited me to join her and a group of friends for supper at a nearby restaurant after the show. I was alone, as was Steve, and I was immediately fascinated by him. In fact, it was love at first sight for me.

One day several years earlier I had approached a session in Los Angeles in a very depressed mood and explained to my analyst that I had just come from a job interview. The producer had offered me a part, but there was something about his personality that upset me very much. He wasn't rude, he wasn't unkind, but he was very cold and business-like, materialistic and insensitive. When I complained to my psychiatrist that this kind of man always depressed me, he explained that my being exposed to such a personality was the equivalent of putting a sensitive microphone in a boiler factory.

I gravitated to the arts, I'm sure, not only because of a love for them but because of an affinity with the sensitive people that one meets in the artistic world. I am repulsed by vulgarity, horrified by rudeness, and terrified of violence. Steve Allen was everything that appealed to me in a man—sensitive, gentle, quiet, calm, introspective, amusing and, of course, handsome.

We were both searching desperately for love, and we were both romantics. A passionate love developed almost immediately, but I refused to marry him unless he, too, sought psychiatric counsel. Our fifteen years together have been rocky at times, but I feel sure that not only would our marriage not have worked but, indeed, we never would even have been attracted to each other had I not already had psychiatric help. Steve's television career was just getting started when we met, and his manager told me on several occasions that he credited our marriage with the blossoming of Steve's tremendous versatility.

I no longer needed a career as an escape. I wanted to embrace life head-on. However, there were still areas to be ironed out, one of which was becoming a mother. As much as I desired a child and loved Steve's three boys by a previous marriage, I was frightened of the responsibility of being a parent myself. Fortunately I was able to work on this problem before little Billy arrived. Mr. Sunshine, as we call him, was almost three years old before he was ever sick, and our pediatrician said, "That is the greatest testimonial to a happy marriage and home-life one can ask for." It's especially rewarding to me when I think back on the many nights I awakened screaming from nightmares concerning childbirth.

I know little or nothing about the world of the psychotic, but I do believe that there are two kinds of neurotics, those who destroy themselves and those who destroy others. It is also my humble opinion that the people I have met who are the most rabidly against psychoanalysis are the very ones who need it the most.

Not everyone, however, can benefit from analysis. It takes courage and an uncompromising honesty, patience, fortitude, and, of course, money. Finding the right psychiatrist is also a difficult problem. For to engage in a relationship as personal as that of stripping bare one's every thought, it is necessary to find an individual with whom one can have genuine empathy.

Life's problems do not miraculously disappear the day one finishes one's analysis. I am constantly looking for danger-signals in moments of emotional crisis. This is a process that I expect to practice until the day I die. I am trying hard to help my nine-year-old face reality and Steve and I agree that we should check the boys every time we see signs of unrealistic thinking.

Five years ago, I was chairman of the fund-raising drive for the National Association of Mental Health. I made many trips for the Association, speaking in ten or twelve different states and on one occasion toured with the late Dr. Will Menninger. I visited the mental institutions and Halfway Houses, addressed legislatures, spoke at universities, and met with many brilliant young doctors who are working in the research field. Next to running my home I consider this the most rewarding and important work I have ever done in my life. Mental illness is not only the number one disease in the United States today, it is on the increase and it is contagious. Such social problems as divorce, homosexuality, dope addiction, crime, alcoholism are rising at an alarming rate. Until we bring the skeleton which is mental illness out of the closet and face facts, we cannot consider ourselves a secure nation. For, no matter how we may want to escape reality, the fact is that our juvenile delinquency problem in the United States has no comparison in the rest of the world.

Psychoanalysis made it possible for me to believe in God with a conviction born of love, not fear. My favorite book, the Bible, asks us: What good is it if you win the world and lose your own soul? Well I say, what good is it if you win the whole world and lose your own child? For our children are what we make them.

A few years ago I spent a day visiting one of the finest mental hospitals in the United States. It was Sunday afternoon and most of the patients were dressed and visiting with friends and relatives. It was sometimes hard to tell the visitors from the patients. But one young girl with the face of a Madonna lurked in the background as we moved from room to room. She appeared to be in her late teens or early twenties and I soon discovered that many of the excellent paintings hanging throughout the hospital were done by her. Other than an obvious shyness and an occasional wringing of hands, she appeared to be completely healthy to me.

When I discussed her case with the doctor, I was told that hers was one of the more difficult in the hospital, since she suffered from intense phobias.

"But surely, doctor," I said, "there must be hope for somebody as young and beautiful and talented as she is." His reply was not optimistic.

I had also been introduced to a ten-year-old blonde boy who reminded me very much of our Billy, and was interested to find that he had the same last name as my mother's family. The little boy followed me around silently all day long, and I was told that he had hardly uttered a word since he had been hospitalized. He, however, must have observed my admiration for the young lady's artistic talents and my obvious pleasure at being given one of her paintings. When it came time for our party to leave the hospital, he dashed out of the room and arrived at the front door carrying a pitiful little drawing which he had made. He presented it to me, and spoke a few words for the first time in many, many months.

The memory of these faces and many more that I have met on my tours for the National Association of Mental Health haunt me, for I know of few physical illnesses as painful as mental illness.

I can't think of a greater investment that any of us can make in the future of this country than to contribute, not just dollars, but our time and our energy to the mental health movement. Most of the mental institutions in this country are still nothing more than warehouses of human misery. I pray that the day is not far off when this great nation of ours, which believes so in freedom and the right of every man to the pursuit of happiness, will find a way to liberate the victims of these institutions.

Psychoanalysis was the turning-point in my life. It was this experience that made it possible for me to grow and go forward as a woman and a human being.

Opening Some Doors
Tennessee Williams
By Don Ross

Tennessee Williams, one of the world's leading playwrights, first went into analysis in 1957, reporting this in an interview with Don Ross, published in the New York Herald Tribune *on January 5, 1958. His father had died that year and his play,* Orpheus Descending *received poor critical notices and closed after a short run. He told Mr. Ross, "I knew I must find help or crack up, so I went to an analyst and poured out all my troubles. I felt the most enormous relief."*

Tennessee Williams disclosed the other night that he is in psychoanalysis. This is of interest to theatergoers because it could mean that a different Williams, a playwright less concerned with distraught people and violence, will eventually emerge. This is what he hopes.

Tuesday, two of Mr. Williams' short plays under the title *Garden District* open at the York Playhouse, First Avenue and

64th Street. The longer of the plays—it is almost a full-length play—is called *Suddenly Last Summer*. It was written during the period, beginning last summer, that Mr. Williams went into analysis. It is violent and shocking, he feels, but it is in a sense a catharsis, a final fling of violence.

"I think if this analysis works it will open some doors for me," said Mr. Williams the other night before a log fire in his New York apartment. He spoke freely, almost eagerly, of his problems as though there were some therapeutic value in unfolding them.

"If I am no longer disturbed myself, I will deal less with disturbed people and with violent material. I don't regret having concerned myself with such people, because I think that most of us are disturbed. But I think I have pretty well explored that aspect of life and that I may be repeating myself as a writer. It would be good if I could write with serenity."

Mr. Williams, a short man with a soft, almost prim mode of speech ("I talk a little pretentiously, don't you think?"), got up to attend to the fire. Smoke was billowing out into the room, and a fine rain of wood ash was settling on him.

"I don't think I'll ever be a bland, comfortable sort of writer," he said. "I think I'll always be a protestant, an outraged romantic, or a Puritan, shocked by things that are reflected in my own character. I don't think I'm more virtuous than the people in my plays that shock me. I'm just as bad or worse."

From his early childhood, Mr. Williams said, he has been neurotic. He is now in his middle forties. He was bothered increasingly by periods of sheer panic in which he feared he would die of a heart attack. He was afflicted by claustrophobia.

He could no longer sit in the middle of a theater with people crowded around him.

He was afraid to walk down a street unless there was a bar in sight—not that he took a drink in each block, but simply because he needed the assurance, in case he panicked, of knowing he could get a drink. A drink was the only thing that could calm him at such times.

Now, after six months in analysis, the fearful spells are much less frequent. He has had only two since the analysis began. (Formerly, he might have as many as twenty in this period of time.) The claustrophobia has subsided. He is more serene. In his apartment house in the East Sixties there is what may be the world's smallest elevator. It holds only one passenger and it gives a rider—or did this rider—the frightening feeling of being in an upended coffin. Mr. Williams is able to step into this conveyance without a twinge of his old claustrophobia.

He spends fifty minutes a day, five days a week, at the office of his analyst. He doesn't intend to become a permanent analysand; he figures that he will give it a year or so.

For years Mr. Williams tried to muddle through without help. Then, a year ago, the last of his plays to appear on Broadway, *Orpheus Descending,* got bad notices and closed after a short run. In it the Williams violence reached a peak: at the close a man was torn to pieces by a pack of dogs.

"I was terribly shocked by its reception," said Mr. Williams. "I had invested so much of myself in it. I had worked longer at it than any other play. I thought it had lyricism, the feeling of tenderness, the striving to understand, the longing, but I did feel that the ending didn't come off quite right.

"I didn't blame the critics or the public. I felt I had failed.

I associated this with the extreme difficulty I had in writing it. *Orpheus* brought all my problems to a head. I knew I must find help or crack up, so I went to an analyst and poured out all my troubles. I felt the most enormous relief." Incidentally, many of Mr. Williams' friends, like Marlon Brando, Elia Kazan, and Irene Selznick had been urging him for a long time to consult a psychoanalyst.

Some people believe that analysis has a bad effect on a writer. "I do not believe this," Mr. Williams said. "If I did I would never have gone into it. I would not hazard or risk my ability to work. I would have preferred to remain confused and troubled. I'm very happy that I had writing as an outlet to my reaction to experience. Otherwise, I would have gone really off my trolley. That's the only thing that saved me."

Like any writer, Mr. Williams is troubled by a fear that he may have said all he has to say. "I believe I wrote my best play early," he said. "It was *A Streetcar Named Desire*. My writing has, I think, followed a declining line since then. My plays have obviously not been as good. I did feel, though, that *Cat on a Hot Tin Roof* brought the line up suddenly. I thought that this was in many ways as good as *Streetcar*. It didn't have its lyric qualities, but the second act was as good as anything I've ever done. With *Orpheus* I felt I was no longer acceptable to the theater public. Maybe, I thought, they'd had too much of a certain dish, and maybe they don't want to eat any more."

Understandably, Mr. Williams does not like to reveal the plot of his plays. But he did say enough about *Suddenly Last Summer* to indicate that it is about a young woman who witnesses the shockingly violent murder of a man. In order to clear herself of suspicion, she tells a story of the death which damages the man's reputation. The man's wealthy and powerful mother has the girl locked up in an insane asylum and, somehow, a psychoanalyst is called in to straighten out the tangle. Mr. Williams believes it is one of his best plays. The other play on the York Theater bill, called *Something Unspoken,* was written five years ago when Mr. Williams was in London.

"It's not a realistic play," said Mr. Williams, of *Suddenly Last Summer.* "The set establishes a non-realistic mood. I hope people will realize it's a moral fable of our times."

The Off-Broadway theater is fine for experimental and controversial works, Mr. Williams thinks. He intends to write other plays for it, but the next thing he has in mind is for Broadway. It's a revision of his *Sweet Bird of Youth,* a full-length play which was produced in Florida a couple of years ago but has not been seen in New York. He hopes to have it ready in August or September.

He has concluded that "Bird's" ending is too violent and threatening and he will tone it down. As it stands now, the hero is emasculated offstage at the end. Mr. Williams will substitute for this physical violence the psychological equivalent of emasculation.

POSTSCRIPT BY LUCY FREEMAN

Mr. Williams first went into analysis in late 1957. At the end of one year, he wrote his mother, Mrs. Edwina Dakin Williams, and his brother, Dakin, a letter in which he said he was discontinuing.

He explained, "I respect the doctor and feel he's done me some good but his fees are too high and if I continue analysis next fall, it will probably be with someone younger and less expensive to go to. Or maybe I won't feel the need of continuing it at all."

In another letter, he wrote his mother about the analyst, "He hit me where it hurt most. He said I wrote cheap melodrama and nothing else."

The Reluctant Hero
By Jim Brosnan

James Patrick Brosnan was a major league pitcher before he turned writer and television commentator. Author of two non-fiction books about the world of baseball, The Long Season *and* Pennant Race, *he is now writing fiction.*

How did I happen to go into psychoanalysis? Because Art Meyerhoff told me to do it.

Art, who later became one of my close friends, is head of his own advertising agency in Chicago and a stockholder in the Chicago Cubs. When I met him, I was eighteen and had been playing in the Cubs' minor league system. It was my first year in organized baseball, what was to be the first of nine lonely years in the minor leagues.

I had started off my career by pitching for Elizabethton, Tennessee, in the Class D Appalachian League where I had won seventeen games and lost eight. Privately, I felt good about that record, but publicly I claimed that with better support I would have won twenty games! Nevertheless I was promoted to another team in the system, Fayetteville, North Carolina, in the Class B Tri-State League. There I ran into trouble.

I was pitching a game and the score was 3-0, with me on the losing end. I threw a ball and and the batter knocked it out of the park for a grand-slam home run. The manager, Frank Scalzi, stalked out to the mound in a fury. He said in a disgusted voice to the other players, "Who wants to pitch?"

Whereupon, I walked away from the mound, out of the ball park and back to my rooming house. I packed my bags and took off for Cincinnati, my hometown. I stayed there six days, nursing the pride wounded by Scalzi's cutting remark, and also feeling a little sorry that I had walked out on the team. Finally I decided to call Jack Sheehan, then head of the Cubs' minor league system.

"Does Scalzi still want me on the team?" I asked.

"Go back and find out," Sheehan advised.

I did. I finished the season with the poor record of two wins and seven losses. I sat by myself most of the time on the bench, disdaining to talk to the other players. I wrote to a friend and described myself thus at this time: "Shortness of temper; unwarranted dislike of people in general; loss of sense of humor, ambition, human understanding."

I found out later that the Cubs' general manager, Jim Gallagher, had gone to Art Meyerhoff, knowing Art was interested in psychoanalysis as well as in the Cubs, and said, "We've got a boy who has great talent but he's also got problems. What do you suggest?"

"Bring him to me," said Meyerhoff.

At Gallagher's suggestion, I went to Art's office on Michigan

Avenue, in the famed Wrigley building. He talked to me about my going into psychoanalysis, for which the Cubs had offered to pay. He didn't convince me I should do so—I was not a convinceable person. I had to convince myself. I tried to tell *him* what psychoanalysis was about. I said I wasn't sure a psychoanalyst could do me any good.

"Why don't you try it?" was all he said.

I said I would think about it.

The season was over, so during that off-season I worked in a warehouse for thirty-five dollars a week, a job Art had got for me. The warehouse was only six blocks from the Chicago Institute for Psychoanalysis where Art had suggested I seek out Dr. George Mohr.

After about a week of work, I decided that if Art thought it was a good idea that I see a psychoanalyst, I would try it. I settled myself in a small room and tried to become accustomed to living on my own for the first time. When I had been playing ball away from home, I felt I was not really on my own, for, in a way, the team took care of me. But now there was no one, and the way I was going, there would never be anyone.

I called up Dr. Mohr and made an appointment to visit him at the Institute. When I first saw him, I was rather disappointed. He seemed too small (I towered over him with my six feet, four inches, and 200 pounds) . I thought psychoanalysts should be more impressive.

Dr. Mohr and I went at it for two months. I didn't know quite what it was all about. I was still playing roles in those days. I didn't know what I was supposed to say, lying there, and he didn't give me any instructions. I was puzzled by the fact that here was a doctor letting me do all the talking and not offering any prescriptions, verbal or otherwise. If there was something wrong with me, I couldn't tell whether he had noticed it, because he would say so very little.

He did not know much about baseball but that was all right with me. I preferred not to talk about baseball outside the ball park. It wasn't until I wrote my books that I felt I could speak or write about baseball without being self-conscious. I didn't want to be thought an expert—I didn't want to be unmasked and revealed as just another scared young pitcher.

I got the impression from Dr. Mohr that he thought continued sessions would be of some help, so I went twice a week at first, then three times a week. I quit after two months, even though there was still a month and a half of the off-season left before I was to report for spring training in Florida. Now that I look back I believe Dr. Mohr was getting fairly close to some things I did not want to talk about. I rationalized my quitting by telling myself that we had reached an impasse, that he wasn't doing me any good. I think, too, knowing that the relationship was a transient one because I had to leave for Florida, I could end it more easily.

I went off for spring training with no discernible progress in analysis as far as I could tell. Or as far as any manager or organization man could tell either. I still had difficulties with managers and umpires and teammates. During this season, my manager, Don Osborn, was a very understanding, patient guy, the first such manager I had encountered. In many subtle ways Osborn encouraged me, both as a ballplayer and as a human being.

I remember that I had said to Art, when he suggested analysis, "What's in it for you, Art?"

Art actually blushed. He didn't know exactly what to say, because I am sure he had not considered what was in it for him, but what was in it for me. But with Osborn, I didn't have that problem. I knew what was in it for him. If he could get me to relax and be more friendly, he would have a better ball team as well as a happier player.

The owners of the team wanted to let me go because they felt I was not really part of the team. I didn't feel I didn't belong, but evidently it seemed obvious to everyone else. I just felt I had a job to do and when it faced me, I did it. When I didn't have a job to do, I just sat on the bench in my own little world. This was a particularly friendly bunch of ball players, more so than any other team for which I had played, but even they couldn't make a dent in my shell of indifference.

We won the Sally League pennant that season so there was a feeling of accomplishment—and even though I wasn't a star, I won nine games and saved four or five. When I returned to Chicago for the off-season, I called Art. I asked if he thought I should try Dr. Mohr again. He, of course, said yes.

So I returned to the office on Michigan Avenue, this time for four months, going three times a week. I did not lie on the couch very often but sat tete-à-tete with Dr. Mohr. It seemed easier to talk that way, and I was beginning to face some of my problems.

I found that now I could discuss myself more freely, especially my feelings about my father. He and I always had a strained relationship. I started to understand that this was the basis for my rebellion against managers, umpires, or any sort of authority.

I always had trouble with umpires. (I see how clearly this is related to my father, who was an umpire for a while.) Once Jocko Conlan, a National League umpire, said to me, "I want to talk to you. Your reputation is bad among umpires."

"Why?" I asked.

"Your attitude is bad," he said. "Why don't you change it? You'll be a better pitcher and get along better with everyone."

If an umpire or manager made a decision I thought unfair, I would blow my stack. This was something I realized I would have to overcome. I believe I've done so. Some of my best friends today are umpires.

It was difficult for me to realize that it was not just one parent who contributed to my lack of cooperation with authorities, but both. I didn't like that at all. You have to have one parent to lean on, and if you feel both are, in a sense, your enemies, you are lost. Dr. Mohr and I discussed my relationship with my mother at quite some length.

I was the oldest of her children, born in Cincinnati on October 24, 1929. I was followed by three younger brothers and two sisters. My father, John, had worked for the Cincinnati Milling Machine Company until he retired, when he became part-time scout for the Reds in the Cincinnati area. He had always wanted to be an umpire. He had been a semi-pro in Ohio for a while, but with his large family he could not afford to live on the salary.

My mother, Rose, a former nurse, was an extremely intelligent woman. She loved music and reading, in contrast to my father whose only interest was baseball. (In time I eventually combined both their interests, becoming both a professional baseball player and a writer.)

I recalled that when I was six or seven years old, I would go to the library every week and pick out books for my mother to read to me. My father would say, "Don't read that junk—read this," and hand me a rule-book on baseball.

I carried out my father's wishes by playing baseball and football as a boy. I saw my first major league game when I was nine years old, the New York Giants against Cincinnati. In high school I grew to six feet one inch, but only weighed 114 pounds so that I looked like a string bean. I pitched for one year at Elder High School, then went out for American Legion baseball. And when I was sixteen, in 1946, I helped pitch the Legion post to the state championship. In the four-state regional and sectional finals, I pitched two shutouts, one a two-hitter, the other a three-hitter. Tony Lucadello, the Chicago Cubs scout, happened to be in the stands watching both games. He came to visit me. "Do you want to play pro ball?" he asked.

I replied that I wanted to go to college but that I didn't have the money. I asked how much it would be worth to him if I turned pro. He left without answering. But he returned two weeks later to sign me to a Cub contract for a bonus of $2500. I had once had ambitions to go into medicine after working at Good Samaritan Hospital in Cincinnati as an X-ray orderly. My mother wanted me to be a doctor; as a nurse, she probably thought that for her son to be a doctor was the highest of all achievements. I had enrolled at Xavier University in Cincinnati as a pre-med student, but quit after one semester because I really was not interested. I far preferred what I was now going to do—join the Cubs farm teams and train in St. Augustine, Florida.

But during that first year, I had created so many problems that Gallagher sent me to Art Meyerhoff, who recommended

Dr. Mohr. And here I was, one year later, back in Dr Mohr's office, trying to look at some of the conflicts I had faced as a boy so I would be able to control myself on the ball field, and get along better with teammates, managers, and umpires.

The last month with Dr. Mohr, during this second period, I reached the point where I could talk about another subject that had been unconsciously troubling me—my sexuality. I was not a dater, had never been. I had indulged in three brief romances, none lasting longer than a month. They were mere flirtations. I had never thought of forming any enduring, intimate relationship with a woman. It was obvious to me that I was not the aggressor, even in my short romances. The women had sought me out as a baseball player. But I was a reluctant hero.

In a way, that was how I felt about my involvement as a ball player. I never felt within myself that I was a baseball star. The picture of me on the bubble gum card never meant anything more than the $125 I got for the endorsement. Even now, I cannot truly understand why my own son shows such idolatry for athletes. I play sports for what's in it for me, like a businessman goes into a certain industry because of what's in it for him.

When I left Dr. Mohr at the end of this second time round, I felt much better about my relationship to him. I liked him more as a person. I felt I had helped him understand me—that was my crowning achievement. Whether I understood myself any better at that particular time is a moot question, although I would guess I did. At least I was now able to have a buddy-buddy relationship with a teammate. Once before, in my first season in the minor leagues, I had a roommate with whom I got along, but he married and, in effect, deserted me.

From then on, I did not try to make friends. In the game of baseball they're here today, gone tomorrow.

As I left Dr. Mohr to go off and play that year in Los Angeles, I felt much warmer toward him. But professionally the whole season turned out to be one disaster after another. I was playing in a league in which I did not belong, for I was technically not ready to compete in it.

I spent the year—my worst in baseball—with four different teams. I started with Springfield, left with a disgraceful 14.14 earned-run average. From there I went to Nashville, then to Des Moines. Once I wrote Art of my difficulties, saying, "Baseball and I are still fighting a battle." Another time I felt differently, writing, "Tonight I go into the game with a determined mind and psychological balance, and for that I thank you."

After I was shipped from Nashville to Des Moines, I became memorably disenchanted with Charley Root, the manager. Root found me in the dressing room, after a tough game which I had lost 1–0, laughing over something I was reading in a magazine. To him, that was the end. The next day I was on my way to Decatur, which is about as low as you can get. Before leaving, Root told me I was the kind of guy who didn't belong in baseball and would never make a success of the game.

Yet at Decatur I found I formed better relationships with the ball players than ever before. They all hated the manager (he's dead now). He was an incompetent who was unable to run the club. Admittedly, we were a bunch of misfits—which is perhaps why we all got along so well. He sent back a description of me to the Cubs which said: "Reported unhappy, still lone wolf. Started off not reporting on time and leaving park after being taken out of the game, but doing little more. . . .

The last time he pitched he walked to the plate in batting practice without cap and, when not at the plate, sat on the bench reading a magazine." All in all I was a sad sack of a pro. When that unhappy season ended, I forgot about baseball. Since I was classified 1-A, I faced a two-year stint in the Army. Instead of spending the off-season time in analysis as I had done before, I decided to go back home to Cincinnati and see my parents. I lived with them for the first time in four years, while waiting for the draft call.

It was then that I started to write. I kept a journal in which I described my feelings. I titled the journal, *Early Broz;* as a record of adolescent misgivings about life it deserves to go unpublished.

But it does mark my first attempt to write, and although consciously I thought I wrote because I didn't have anything else to do, I realize that there was some carry-over from my analysis.

With Dr. Mohr not available, I was trying a kind of self-analysis. With him in the room, I had been able to speak my thoughts. Without him, I could put them down on paper.

Before, I had spent my time reading. But now, instead of reading, I was writing. The experience was almost as rewarding as playing baseball.

I spent two years in the Army, and never left Fort Meade, Maryland, where I played for the post baseball team. Thanks to the help Dr. Mohr had given me, I could accept the authority of the Army. I realized I couldn't rebel against it so I rode with it, and there was no fighting. Again, due to the help Dr. Mohr had given me, I found that after I entered the Army my relationships with women were far freer. He helped me break down my barriers against sexual involvement. We would talk about the difference between love and sex, and how sex could be part of love, but that without love, or an appreciation or understanding of the woman, sex meant little.

One night at a party I met a very attractive young woman named Anne Stewart Pitcher who came from Virginia and worked at Fort Meade. Anne and I discovered we had at least two things in common, baseball and music. As a boy, I played the trombone and later the piano, and had always liked classical music, especially Bartok. Anne not only liked music but was an avid baseball fan. To her, I was a hero. And now, to myself, I was not such a reluctant one. We were married six months later on June 23, 1952.

Marriage is not always an easy relationship. I think Anne should have gotten a medal for her patience and understanding over the years.

A year after our marriage, I was out of the Army and back in baseball, pitching once again for Springfield, now a triple-A ball team. I won four games, lost seventeen and decided, with that abysmal record, to quit baseball. That summer I took an Army aptitude test. It showed I would be proficient either at statistics or writing. The latter offered little security so, in the winter of 1953, I enrolled for a two-year course in accounting at a school in Washington.

I was doing well, passing all subjects with good grades, when I unaccountably got a notice that my contract had been bought by the Cubs. Chicago was so hard up for pitchers that they were even willing to try me.

That spring I made the team. But I wasn't with the Cubs long before I was shipped to Beaumont in the Texas

League. I found myself surprisingly relaxed, however. I started to throw a slider. Before that, all I had was a curve that didn't curve very much, and a fast ball that really wasn't very fast. But at Beaumont, I chalked up a seven wins, one loss record, and felt things had started to improve at last.

The breaks did begin to come my way. And with each succeeding good break, I relaxed even more. I didn't repeat my mistakes as often, although I still made them.

After three years of marriage, Anne and I had our first baby, and I had a really good year. It may be coincidental that the baby was born in the same year I had such a good season, but I do know that I had a much more relaxed relationship with one person—my wife.

I also started to find friends among my teammates, no matter where I was playing. The turning point came when I was pitching for Los Angeles of the Pacific Coast League.

Jamie had just been born and, like most new fathers, I thought constantly about our baby. On the road, I did what I always did—read or attended a foreign movie by myself. The other guys still resented "The Professor," as they called me, although I don't think I have ever acted like an intellectual snob. As Billy Martin, one of my ex-teammates at Cincinnati put it, "Some guys got a college education, they try to lord it over us. We call them intellectual stupes. Broz is very well educated, but acts just like a regular guy."

There came a day when I got into a tight ball game against Oakland. In the eighth inning, I had a 2–0 lead. One runner was on base. I threw the ball and the batter, George Metkovich, connected with it. It sailed out to deep right field, a fly. It should have been caught, but a boy in the bleachers reached out with a glove and snatched the ball away from the outfielder. The umpire ruled it a home run. The score was tied.

The game went into a tenth inning. Then, with a man on second, one of the Oakland players hit a ground ball. It struck a pebble and bounced over the second baseman's head. The winning run came across the plate.

After the game, I went to the lockers, raging mad. My brother, Jerry, a high school teacher in San Francisco, was visiting me. He walked into the dressing room and suggested we go out for dinner. Much to my surprise, I heard myself saying to him "No, I'm going out and get drunk."

At the first bar, I downed two double Gibsons. I traveled to a second bar, then a third. I vaguely remember running into two Oakland players somewhere along the way and waving at them, something I had never done.

"What the hell's wrong with Broz?" I heard one of them ask.

They each bought me a drink. By that time I was weaving slightly, so they helped me into a taxi, directing the driver to take me to the airport so I would not miss the plane the rest of the team was taking. At the airport, I headed immediately for the lounge and another drink, and there found three of my teammates. They stared at me in astonishment as I lurched in, and promptly bought me drinks.

By then I was almost out cold and had to be helped onto the plane. I don't remember a thing about that trip back to Los Angeles. All I know is that half a dozen of my teammates carried me off the plane. Anne was standing inside the gate, waiting. She took one look at me, turned her back, and walked away.

Bob Scheffing, the Los Angeles manager, sent the Cubs' front office a report of the incident. It simply said: "Brosnan finally joined the ball club."

I suddenly became a better pitcher. I won nine of my last twelve games and finished the season with seventeen wins and ten losses and a 2.38 earned-run average. The next year saw me in the majors for keeps.

This was the start of a pretty good relationship with teammates, managers—and umpires. I began to understand managers a little better, because I found I could put myself in their place and consider their problems. The Cubs were constantly shifting managers and the managers, I realized, seemed to have more problems than I did. At long last, I wasn't one of their problems.

I saw Art Meyerhoff throughout these years and occasionally we would talk about Dr. Mohr and how grateful we felt for his help. Art made no secret of the fact that he, too, had gone to Dr. Mohr for analysis.

Between 1955 and 1962, I was accepted as a big league baseball player, although not as anything more than a fairly competent pitcher. For a time, I worried about this. I thought that perhaps I was not physically strong enough to become any better. I went to the physical research laboratory at the University of Illinois where Dr. T. K. Cureton, the head of the laboratory, gave me a battery of tests. At the end, he told me, "You have the physique of an average fan, not an athlete's body."

Dr. Cureton set up an exercise program for me and by the end of it, I was in good shape to play ball. "Better than the average fan," he assured me.

I now became an aggressive player who wanted to prove he

could win for any ball club. And the Cubs immediately traded me to the Cardinals.

This might have proved a setback psychologically except that I automatically received a raise.

While with the Cubs, I had started to keep a diary at the suggestion of Bob Boyle, a magazine writer who became a friend of mine. I showed Boyle the diary after I was traded to the Cardinals, and he became so enthusiastic about it that he showed it to *Sports Illustrated* which decided to publish it.

That started me on my writing career in earnest. While with the Cardinals, I wrote a series of articles for the *St. Louis Post-Dispatch* about our team's trip to Japan. I also started to write fiction, including a sympathetic story of a manager as a guy with problems (never published, although bought).

The next season I was traded to the Cincinnati Reds. I kept pitching, and writing. *Sports Illustrated* asked me to write more articles and suggested I come to New York for a talk. I had an hour's wait for the train home, and decided to call Evan Thomas, editor at *Harper & Row*, a name suggested to me by Boyle. I asked Mr. Thomas if he thought *Harper & Row* would be interested in a book based on the article I hade done for *Sports Illustrated*. He said they would.

Things were really looking up now. We had our second child, a boy, Timmie. My first year with the Reds was a good one. I appeared in fifty-seven games, pitched ninety-nine innings, won seven games, lost two, and finished third in the National League in earned-run average with 2.36.

We won the pennant in 1961 and I played in the World Series which made it a big year for me professionally. My first book, *The Long Season*, sold over 20,000 copies. Jimmy Cannon called it "The greatest baseball book ever written," and the late great humorist James Thurber said, "When it comes to writing, Brosnan has a good fast ball and a dazzling curve."

Some of my teammates were not quite sure what to think about my writing. Before I was traded to the Reds, in Florida the Cardinal manager, Solly Hemus, who had read some of the magazine articles taken from the book, said sarcastically to a visitor, "You think Brosnan's writing was funny? Wait till you see him pitch."

Yet in spite of all my good luck, I wasn't particularly happy. I could not understand why, when I had reached the pinnacle of my career as a baseball player and had started off well as a writer, I still felt depressed.

I decided to go back into analysis. Dr. Mohr had left Chicago to live and practice in Los Angeles. My new analyst was a woman, Dr. Lucia Tower, whose offices were also at the Institute. I saw her during the off-season of 1961 for about three months, twice a week. She helped me through my depression. She encouraged me to write my second book and to try fiction and poetry which I had long wanted to do, as well as to write about subjects other than sports.

The help given me, first by Dr. Mohr and then by Dr. Tower, has, I feel, allowed me to communicate first, with myself, second, with Anne, and finally, with other people.

I have stopped playing professional baseball and have been conducting a television program about the sports scene in Chicago. As an interviewer, I have had my best success encouraging people to talk about themselves. Without the help I received in the analysts' offices, I don't think I could have done this.

Nor could I have written my first book. Or my second, *Pennant Race*. And now, as I write the book of fiction I have always wished to write, I do it with the knowledge that I am not afraid to tackle it, no matter what the outcome.

In looking back, I feel that my analysis, my marriage, and knowing Art Meyerhoff were the most important steps I took toward a fuller, more satisfying life. I have reached an understanding of myself and know now that people are good to know for what they are, and not for what I am to them or can get out of them.

From Buddha To Freud
By Bud Freeman

Bud Freeman is one of the jazz "greats." Born in Chicago, he became a member of the Austin High group which spread the best of jazz to the world. Today, he is considered by jazz authorities to be one of the greatest living tenor saxophonists. He is kept busy composing, making recordings, appearing by invitation in far corners of the world, and taking part in all the leading jazz festivals.

Several years ago a woman with whom I was very much in love died quite suddenly. Her death plunged me into a deep state of shock. In spite of all the romances in my life (after all, I was a jazz musician and a world traveler), I do not recall that I was ever in love before. Surely not this completely.

Since sorrow to me is a private affair, I could not visualize myself crying out to my friends no matter how bereft I felt. I spent several months gripped by an emotional paralysis, not knowing how to extricate myself from this grief.

One night, coming home quite late from a concert in Westport, Connecticut, I caught a taxicab from Grand Central to my hotel-home in Greenwich Village. The driver was a soft-spoken Negro in his late fifties. We struck up the usual casual cab conversation. However, in the few words we exchanged, he seemed so warm and friendly that I broke down and told him about my devastating loss.

When I finished my story, there was silence. Then he turned around and said to me in that soft-spoken voice, "Young man," (this compliment in itself was enough to stir me out of my shock) "have you ever heard of Lao-Tsu?"

I confessed I had not. He explained that Lao-Tsu was a famous Chinese philosopher who lived about 600 years before Christ. He said, "I suggest you get a book of his writings called *The Way of Life*."

We had by then arrived in front of my hotel but instead of accepting the fare and dismissing me to seek further business, he turned off his meter, parked the cab, and sat and talked for about an hour. I remember him saying, "I can understand the sorrow and shock you feel, but *you* have to live."

Our conversation lifted my depressed spirit. When he said goodnight, I went to my apartment and lay awake most of the night thinking about what he had said. As soon as I awakened, I called the Washington Square Bookshop and asked my friend, Lois, if she had *The Way of Life* in stock.

"I can get it for you in a day or so, Bud," she said.

The book was so fascinating that I could not understand how, with all the reading I'd done in my life, I could have missed it. Lao-Tsu led me to another book called *Zen Buddhism* which I found even more interesting. It was written by the great Suzuki who, incidentally, is still alive and lives in Ipswich, Massachusetts, I believe. I found myself spending three or four hours a day in my hotel room reading the pages over and over, completely entranced by the words and thoughts. They led me to a quest for more and more books about Buddhism and ultimately Zen Buddhism.

It seemed to me that all the books stressed one point—the need to rid oneself of false values. I realized that, in the past, I had lived in such an egomaniacal shell that I thought of the world and me as two separate things. I now began to see that I was a part of the world, rather than apart from the world.

I had always thought I was too important to call agents for work, but thinking about one of the profound Lao-Tsu epigrams—if you never assume importance, you never lose it—I decided to call a man who was the head of a recording company.

I simply said to him, "This is Bud Freeman. I'd like to make an album for you."

And he simply said, "Bud Freeman! Of course. For Christ's sake, where the hell have you been?"

And I answered, "I've just stepped out of my shell."

The following day I casually telephoned an agent. I told him I would like to take a group out on the road.

"Let me make some phone calls and I'll get back to you tomorrow," he said.

Three hours later he telephoned and asked whether I would like to play at a nightclub near Philadelphia called the Petti Arms. I would have to open in three days. Since the job came so suddenly, I asked him to suggest some jazz musicians who had been working for him.

One of them turned out to be Buddy Blacklock, a fine pianist and, incidentally, a fine painter. Buddy is a very interesting person and in the short time we worked together, we became good friends.

One day he asked, "Bud, would you mind if I asked my wife to come down for a couple of days?"

"For God's sake, why do you have to ask me?" I said. "Of course, have her come."

"It's just that some band leaders don't like to have wives around," he explained.

Buddy's wife, Lauren, arrived from New York the next day and I took them both to lunch at a little diner near Swarthmore College. Lauren was delightful, and the three of us spent several hours over lunch getting acquainted. Lauren writes very lovely poetry and is also a painter. I was impressed to find that she had a complete collection of my early records, a number of which I could not even recall having made.

As we were leaving the diner, Lauren turned to Buddy and asked, "Don't you think Mother and Bud would enjoy knowing each other?"

I thought, "Who the hell wants to meet somebody's mother?" But, of course, I said, "I'd like very much to meet her."

After several broken dates on both sides, we finally got together. (I later found out that Fay had little interest in meeting a jazz musician). When you speculate about a married woman's mother, you are apt to conjure up the picture of a woman who is not particularly young or attractive.

But Fay turned out to be not only young but most attractive. She was a blonde with expressive blue eyes that held both depth and sparkle. She moved with the grace of a modern dancer, which she was. She also painted. But her regular job was working with children of above average intelligence who had difficulty in learning.

After several dates I knew I was in love with Fay. But the thought of marriage terrified me. I tried to explain it to her. "I can't even handle the chaos in my own life, let alone take on the chaos of living with someone else."

Very quietly, very softly, she asked, "Would you like to see a psychiatrist?"

"I really don't have much faith in that sort of thing," I said. "I think it's just a racket. I haven't met anyone who has been helped by it."

Fay did not argue the point. With her understanding, she realized people cannot be cajoled, coerced, or commanded to go into treatment.

It took about a month after Fay's gentle suggestion to decide that perhaps I should make an appointment with a therapist. Because of Fay's work, she is in constant consultation with people in the profession, so she asked for a recommendation and was given the name of a psychiatrist whom I shall call Dr. Hanid.

I called Dr. Hanid to ask for an appointment. I liked his voice. It had a warm ring.

When I arrived at the interview, I saw a well-dressed, graceful man of about forty. He looked as if he had just stepped out of the pages of *Esquire,* yet his speech had none of the smugness you would expect to accompany this kind of appearance.

I immediately reminded him that I was much older than he. His answer was quick and direct. "You may have seen many things in life that I have not seen but I know more about what you need than you do."

I expected to feel awkward and embarrassed during our first meeting, since I thought of myself as highly neurotic. Instead, I found a very relaxed, reassuring man who made me feel very comfortable. I almost reached the point of loving myself during that hour. I was delighted to learn that the eminent Dr. Hanid liked jazz and was well aware of my work and was a fan. I was later to find that not every session was so pleasant. There were difficult days. *He* was never difficult but I thought he was. Sometimes I fought him as though he were the enemy —not I.

After a few sessions I was delighted to find that I wasn't as crazy as I thought I was. I had a regular appointment once a week and I have kept it for the past five years, except when I am out of the city or the country. I am still very much interested in the Buddhistic teachings but now feel that psychotherapy has been more beneficial. In spite of all we may read about how we should feel and act, we can never really find out about ourselves from the pages of a book.

It is not easy to talk freely about oneself to a stranger. Sometimes Dr. Hanid would challenge me angrily, hoping to open me up. After a session of this kind, I would walk out of his office saying to myself, "I'll never speak to that bastard again," but then, after thinking about what he said during the following week, I was always eager to get back for the next appointment to tell him how wrong I was.

I had difficulty describing my feelings about what was happening in my life. I didn't want to face certain things. Several times I arrived at his office and announced that I was psychologically fit and I didn't think I needed further therapy. I added the excuse that I couldn't afford it. I do not play nightclubs, and in the concert field, if a musician plays a couple of concerts a week, he is doing extremely well. But the truth of the matter was that I was not ready to face certain fears—the fear of getting married, the fear of having to take care of someone else.

People believe there's a mystique in unveiling the mind. There isn't. It's simply a matter of hard, honest, cold questioning of one's self.

Gradually I was able to tell him things I always thought were embarrassing. After a few months of therapy, I discovered I had suddenly acquired the courage to marry Fay. Not that it took courage to marry her, for she is a darling, loving woman. But it took courage for me to divorce myself from myself.

We were married on a beautiful, sunny day in June of 1960 by a Unitarian minister in a small chapel in a Park Avenue church.

At this writing, I have been in therapy for five years. I am still with Dr. Hanid and, I hope, less of a dilemma both to him and to me.

Living has become less complex as a result of my therapy. I no longer am driven to stay up all hours of the night. When I am not working, I go to bed early. Fay rises early because of her work, and I now enjoy getting up with her.

In looking back at my bachelor life, I cannot imagine being single again. To me, the only life is the married life.

Dr. Hanid is never one to dissect the obvious. When I would occasionally question, "Why? What makes me like this? What happened in my past?" he would immediately reply, almost sarcastically, that I was not in psychoanalysis but in psychotherapy. And then he would add, "But if you insist, your mother loved you too much!" It always reminded me of the great Ring Lardner line, " 'Aw shut up,' he explained."

Certainly psychotherapy has helped me to overcome many of my fears. One day I complained to Dr. Hanid that I didn't like the picture I presented to the audience as I stood playing the saxophone, my cheeks bursting so that my face appeared puffy and distorted. My sense of vanity was hurt.

He pointed out that the audience did not come there to admire my physiognomy.

"Oh," I said, in sudden awareness. "You mean the audience doesn't come to listen to my face."

Another fear was that I would not play my instrument well as I grew older. This unrealistic fear seems to have vanished. Now, with new confidence and trust in myself, I find, and I think the critics agree, that I am playing better than ever.

I shall be sixty on my next birthday. My hope now is that I will play the horn until they place it on top of me.

The Alien Voice Within
By Hermann Hesse

The late Hermann Hesse, winner of the Nobel Prize for literature, who died in 1962, wrote an essay in 1918, in which he discussed the effect of psychoanalysis on the creative spirit. Translated from the original German by Miriam M. Reik, it appeared in the Psychoanalytic Review, Vol. 50, No. 3, Fall of 1963.

TRANSLATOR'S INTRODUCTION by Miriam M. Reik

In 1918 Hermann Hesse (1877-1962) wrote an essay, remarkable both for its time and in itself, on the relationship between the creative work of the artist and the then very new analytic depth psychology. "Künstler und Psychoanalyse," the full text of which is here translated for the first time, was written when Hesse was 41 years old, before the publication of his best novels. *Demian* had not yet appeared, *Siddhartha* and *Der Steppenwolf* had not yet been written, and it was not to be until 1946 that *Das Glasperlenspiel* (published under the English title, *Magister Ludi*) would win him the Nobel Prize for literature.

Hesse's acquaintance with psychoanalysis stemmed not only from fairly extensive reading in its literature but, as the remarks in his essay clearly indicate, from personal experience. The poet was apparently suffering from symptoms of a compulsion neurosis, when a personal emotional crisis brought him to consult a psychoanalyst in Switzerland in 1916. Whatever the nature of the treatment—which seems to have been rather unorthodox—it shortly bore artistic fruit in the intensely self-analytic *Demian,* while the present article offers another, nonfictional commentary on that period.

Hesse's essay is a greeting to the psychoanalyst from the German romantic spirit, a greeting which demonstrates little of the ambivalence toward the science which other writers have at times expressed. Like Thomas Mann, he profited from finding in psychoanalysis what he regarded as a living philosophy of inward phantasy, an insight into the relation between myth and fiction. Hesse felt particularly at one with the science of psychoanalysis in its moral aspect, in the undeviating search for inner truth.

But most important to Hesse was the fact that psychoanalysis allowed him to experience the raw materials of the mind, which seemed to confirm for him certain ideas about the way in which the primitive and instinctual exist in relation to reason and the intellect, and how this relationship produces those synthetic representations which we call the realm of the imagination. These ideas are expressed in Hesse's essay in the form of a pseudobiological concept of the history of evolution, and also as a profound sense of identification with the life of all the universe.

However, it is in Hesse's novels, in his world of religious symbols and dramatic psychological transfigurations, that these concepts are fully elaborated. There one sees the unconscious, imperative and mysterious agents of human life operating as a source of infinite renewal for the individual who is destroyed by the asceticism of the spirit (as in *Siddhartha* or Joseph Knecht). Hesse also perceived the unconscious as a source of human solidarity against a society encrusted by conventions.

Hesse's discussion of psychoanalysis is thus in literary-philosophic terms and presented from the viewpoint of the artist. But there is no reason to wish that he had made concessions to the language of the psychoanalytic formalist or to the canons of presentation. As he suggests, the relationship between the artist and psychoanalyst is, so to speak a symbiotic one, and by retaining the speech of the poet he is plainly upholding his part of that relationship.

It was to be expected that the artist especially would take kindly to psychoanalysis, this new, so variously fruitful way of looking at things. Very many might have interested themselves in psychoanalysis as neurotics, to be sure. But beyond that, the artist was more inclined and prepared to become involved with a psychology placed on entirely new foundations than with the official science. The artist is always more easily won over to the highly gifted radical than is the professor.

For the individual artist then, to the extent to which he was not content with the issue as a new theme for discussion to be taken into the coffee house, there quickly arose the effort to learn as an artist from the new psychology—even more, there arose the question of if and how far the new psychological understanding could be of any good for creativity itself.

In its application to poetic work as well as in the observation of daily life, the fruitfulness of the new science is evidently proven. We now have one more key—no absolute, magical key, but still a valuable attitude, a superior new instrument whose serviceability and trustworthiness have quickly demonstrated themselves. I am not thinking in this connection of particular literary-historical efforts which could make detailed case histories out of the lives of the poets. Rather, the corroboration and correction of Nietzche's psychological insights and of his finely sensitive conjectures has been in itself exceedingly valuable to us. The initial knowledge and observation of the unconscious, of the meaning of psychic mechanisms such as repression, sublimation, regression, and so on, has yielded a clear schema which is immediately enlightening.

While psychology has now become familiar and easily accessible to everybody, the utility of this psychology for the artist remains rather doubtful. As little as historical science can make one capable of writing historical fiction, as little as botany or geology can help in describing a landscape, so little can the best scientific psychology help to portray man. Indeed, one saw how the psychoanalysts themselves everywhere made use of the poetry of pre-analytic times as confirmations, sources and testimonials. Thus, what analysis recognized and formulated scientifically, had always been known by the poets. The poet has shown himself as representative of a particular way of thinking which is really the complete contrary of the analytic-psychological way. He was the dreamer, the analyst was the interpreter of his dreams. Can anything remain for the poet, even granting all his interest in the new psychology, other than to continue dreaming and to follow the call of his unconscious?

No, nothing else remains for him. All of analysis cannot make him into an interpreter of the soul who was no poet before, who had not felt the inner frame and heartbeat of the emotional life. With it, he could only apply a new scheme, could perhaps baffle for a moment, but he could not essentially enhance his powers. The poetic grasp of emotional processes remains, after as before, a thing of intuitive, not analytic talents.

However, the question is not thereby settled. The path of the psychoanalyst can, in fact, also be of advantage to the artist. However wrong he would be to take analytic technique over into the artistic sphere, yet he would be right to regard psychoanalysis seriously and to follow it. I see three corroborations and confirmations which proceed to the artist from analysis.

First, the profound confirmation given to the value of phantasy or fiction. Whenever the artist views himself analytically, it does not remain hidden from him that among the weaknesses from which he suffers is a mistrust of his calling; a doubt of phantasy; an alien voice within him which gives assent to the bourgeois attitude and education and which wants to evaluate all his activity as "only" a pretty fiction. Yet, analysis impressively teaches every artist that it is precisely what he could sometimes assess as "only" a fiction which is of the highest value, and it emphatically reminds him of the existence of fundamental emotional demands as well as of the relativity of all authoritarian measurements and evaluations. Analysis endorses the artist before himself. It simultaneously offers him a free region of pure intellectual activity in analytic psychology.

This use of the method will already be experienced by him who is only acquainted with it from the outside. The two other values offer themselves only to those who have undergone depth analysis seriously and thoroughly themselves, and to whom it is not an intellectual matter but becomes a living experience. The most important values escape him who is content to receive some enlightenment about his own "complex" and then to learn some information that can be formulated about his inner life.

He who has earnestly gone some distance on the path of analysis through memory, dreams and associations in search of the primary spiritual sources retains as an enduring benefit what could perhaps be called "more intimate terms with his own unconscious." He experiences a warmer, more fruitful, more passionate back-and-forth between the conscious and unconscious; he takes what otherwise remains "under the threshold" and what is only enacted in unnoticed dreams, and transfers much of it with him into the light.

And this again is intimately related to the significance of psychoanalysis for ethics, for personal conscience. The analyst, before all others, makes a great, fundamental demand whose circumvention and neglect is soon punished, and whose sting penetrates very deeply and leaves lasting traces. It demands a sincerity towards oneself to which we are not accustomed. It teaches us to see, to acknowledge, to explore, and to take seriously exactly that which we have most successfully repressed. With the first steps one takes in analysis, this is already a powerful, even prodigious experience; a shaking down to the roots. He who holds his ground and goes further, sees himself only more isolated from step to step, more cut off from convention and traditional views; he sees himself compelled to ask and to doubt and not to stop before anything. Instead, he sees or suspects more and more of the inexorable image of the truth of nature emerging behind the collapsing traditions. Only in the intensive self-examination of analysis is a part of the history of evolution really experienced and pervaded with full-blooded emotion. Going back to mother and father, peasant and nomad, ape and fish, nowhere is the origin, relatedness and hope of man so earnestly and shakingly experienced as in a serious analysis. What you have learned will become visible, what you have known will become heartbeats, and when the anxieties, embarrassments and repressions are lifted, the significance of life and of personality is the more pure, more imperative matter.

This educational, demanding, stimulating power of analysis is not felt by any to more advantage than by the artist. The most comfortable adjustment to the world and its customs is not important to him, but rather the singular thing which he himself represents.

Among the poets of the past, some came very close to understanding the essential tenets of analytic depth psychology. The closest was Dostoyevski, who not only intuited those roads which Freud and his students would travel long before them, but who also possessed a true practice and technique of this kind of psychology. Among the great German poets is Jean Paul, whose concept of emotional processes stands closest to those of today. Besides that, Jean Paul is the most splendid example of the artist whose permanent, intimate contact with his own unconscious, emerging from profound, living presentiments, becomes an infinitely productive well-spring.

In concluding, I quote a poet whom we are accustomed to count among the pure idealists, but not among the dreamers or introverted natures, and who, all in all, belongs more to the intensely intellectual poets. Otto Rank was first to discover in the following passage of a letter one of the most amazing premodern confirmations of the psychology of the unconscious. Schiller wrote to Körner, who complained of having trouble with his productiveness: "The reason for your complaint, it seems to me, lies in the coercion imposed upon your imagination by your intellect [*Verstand*]. It does not seem good, and it is detrimental to the creative work of the soul when the intellect passes review too sharply over the stream of ideas, like a watch-man. Considered in isolation, an idea can be very insignificant and very adventurous, but can perhaps become weighty through one which follows it; it can form a very important member in a certain connection with others. It seems to me that intellect, in a creative mind, has withdrawn its sentinel from the gates. The ideas stream in pêle-mêle, and only then will the intellect look them over and examine the great heap."

Here is the classical expression of the ideal relation between the intellectual critic and the unconscious. Neither the repression of the material which emerges from out of the unconscious, of uncontrolled ideas, dreams, playful phantasy, nor continued surrender to the shapeless eternality of the unconscious, but the loving listening to the hidden springs and only then criticism and selection from the chaos—this is the way every great artist has worked. If any technique can help fulfill this demand, then it is psychoanalysis.

Man With -- and Without -- Camera
By Ken Heyman

Ken Heyman is a photo-journalist whose work has appeared in all the leading magazines. At one time, he was under contract to Life *and he later was a member of Magnum. He has exhibited in museums throughout the world. His photographs have appeared frequently in American photographic annuals.*

Mr. Heyman's book, Family, *with accompanying text by Margaret Mead, was published with great success in 1965. Among his most recent books are* This America, *with former President Johnson;* The Color of Man; *and* The Private World of Leonard Bernstein.

I was a nothing, a nobody. I had no future and I didn't care. When I looked into a mirror all I saw was hair that needed combing or where the shaving cream ended when I put the razor to my face . . . I didn't exist. With no confidence, I could hardly decide what I wanted for dinner.

That was in 1951, when I was a sophomore at Columbia University. I was failing most of my subjects, but I didn't care.

The future was unbearable, and photography was an escape. Between relationships with girls and processing my pictures in the darkroom, there was little time for study. Often I would develop and print while listening to Vivaldi or Mozart on the radio. Printing until three or four in the morning, I would then sleep through most of my morning classes.

Today I realize this preoccupation with photography did not embody a desire to become a photographer, but was a running away from my responsibilities as a student. In December, 1951, I was put on scholastic probation, and in January, 1952, at the time of the Korean War, I was drafted into the Army.

The summer before I was drafted, I was considering photography more seriously. I took a course at one of the better photography schools in New York. I lasted eleven days. When the instructor kicked me out, he informed me that I wasn't serious enough about my work.

I then took an art course at Columbia. It was a course that involved no homework, which appealed to me. I got the only F in the class and was asked not to return.

Apparently, at no time during my school or college training, did I display any special creative abilities. Because I possessed a high I.Q., the teachers made it doubly difficult. They knew I could do better and they felt I was just lazy. (It seems a shame that more is not done to help young people who might be creative but who get lost in the maze of the educational process.)

At an early age, I learned to *see* and not be heard. If I did venture a feeble opinion, my brothers or my father would immediately "jump on me" and tell me I was wrong, that I didn't know what I was talking about. It didn't take long for me to accept what they knew, and to think that I didn't know what I was talking about . . . so I just sat back and watched.

I gave up photography for three years when I went into the Army, believing that it was only my way of escaping responsibilities. A month after I was discharged, I was back at Columbia as a GI veteran. I hadn't the vaguest idea of what I wanted to be, and I guess I knew I needed help. As a last resort I asked Dr. Marion Kenworthy, a longtime friend of the family, and a prominent psychoanalyst, what I should do. She referred me to another psychoanalyst and I started analysis, going five times a week.

It was difficult at first. For months I was unable to talk about my parents or separate them as individuals. My analyst wanted to hear about dreams and because it was hard to discuss basic problems, I brought in many dreams. I dreamed a great deal and could bring in as many as five for one session. There were so many that there wasn't time to work out their meanings. However, over the years I've learned the value of dreams, and understand their meaning. Today, they often reveal a problem that has been bothering me, or suggest a solution that hasn't occurred to my conscious mind.

I've often wondered how much psychoanalysis has helped me. It's difficult to answer because I don't know what I'd be if I hadn't gone, certainly not what I am today. Now I'm a whole person; a living, breathing, and most important, *feeling* person.

As a child I had tremendous defenses, so much so that nothing reached me. I had sealed off my emotions from the outside world . . . I couldn't be hurt. Analysis has unlocked this door.

I've learned to appreciate and live with my feelings.

At one point the question arose: If you are a creative artist, won't psychoanalysis hurt your work? I can only answer for myself. I'm convinced that liberating my emotions, freeing my inhibitions, has helped enormously. In my kind of photography I have to react with complete spontaneity to the minutest cue from my subjects. Because I've learned a great deal about myself and have been able to apply much of this to my work, it's almost given me an unfair advantage over other photographers.

I've come a long way from the weeks at Columbia, of hiding in my tiny apartment under the guise of a depression. Today, I work hard at photography. I suppose I work equally hard at having a healthy, happy family. I met Wendy, my wife, at a dinner party. I was more interested in her as a lovely, sensitive person than in the fact that she was a soap-opera queen. She was playing one of the two lead roles, the part of Ellen, in "As the World Turns," still the leading daytime television serial.

We went out during the next ten months, always accompanied by her TV script. Before we could have dinner, Wendy had to learn her lines for the next day's show.

We were married on September 11, 1960. Our oldest child, Jennifer, was born precisely nine months and ten minutes after we were married. We have three other children, all boys.

I've learned through analysis not to be ashamed of my emotions but to use them in my work.

When I photograph, I don't exist. If the camera had a long cable release, I would want the subject I'm photographing to take his own picture. I try to be as responsive to my subject as possible. My training with Margaret Mead, while at Columbia and while working with her in Bali, Mexico, and New York, in addition to my psychoanalytic background, has helped me look at situations as though I have never experienced them. In other words, for me the best photographic technique is to consider every situation a completely new experience.

I have certain clues as to how well I'm working. My physical involvement is one clue to my mood. When I begin photographing people (I'm always photographing people), I find that if I'm working well, I will go immediately to the proper vantage point. It may be lying on the floor, squatting, or climbing up on something. But if I'm not working well, I just keep my 35 mm. camera at eye level in a standing position at my six-foot, one-inch height, and walk around taking only the pictures that are necessary.

I never carry a camera when I'm not working because I'm not functioning then as a photographer but as a human being. When I'm a photographer, I'm a different kind of animal, usually tense, restless, and occasionally aggressive.

My best photographs occur when I'm away from home. I've learned to use my loneliness, to allow it to work for me. My working habits "on the road" include photographing and studying people continuously. At that time, I don't enjoy meeting people socially, or being entertained, if it has nothing to do with getting the job done.

I want to know everything about the people I photograph and the situations with which I'm working. I ask endless questions—who they are and what they are. Many of the questions are more personal than people are used to discussing. I feel my photography is just an extension of this finding out, of exploring and meeting people.

In *Family,* when I photographed a mother with a child, I wanted not only to photograph motherhood, but to try and squeeze out all that I could about the way *that* mother felt about *her* child.

I'm not certain that psychoanalysis is the reason that there is little resemblance between who I am today and who I was ten years ago, but I can't think of a better one.

Sink or Swim
Patty Duke
By Rex Reed

In an interview with Rex Reed, carried in the drama section of The New York Times *on Sunday, Nov. 3, 1968, Patty Duke, movie and television star, spoke of how she felt when, at the age of eighteen, she married director Harry Falk, who was thirty-two and divorced, and decided to retire for a while.*

I had decided to sink or swim and I was sinking. I felt emotionally unequipped to take care of a man. I had worked all my life as a kid actor, then suddenly I wasn't one any more. I was married and a homemaker. It was what I chose, yet I didn't know how to *be* one, I didn't even know how to cook. I wasn't holding up my end of the bargain and I needed someone to talk to. So I went to a psychiatrist. That took guts, but I'm glad I went. It's nothing to be ashamed of. If you break a toe, you go to a doctor, right? So if you have something wrong in your head, you gotta get help or it gets worse. Analysis is a lot better than pills. I learned where my problems were coming from. As a kid, I had days when I did nothing but cry for nine hours straight. If I blew a line, I worried that people wouldn't like me. It was that fantastic drive to be liked because I was so insecure. Hell, I was just a child, for God's sake, and what do kids know? They just want to be accepted and liked by everybody. Analysis taught me how to laugh. When I was a child I wasn't impressed by anybody. The only person I ever met who impressed me was John F. Kennedy. Now I have more compassion for people. I don't have such a high opinion of *me* any more, because I have more important things to work out than the drive to succeed.

I was very poor when I was little and if I hadn't become a child star, I don't know what I would have been. I might have turned into a prostitute or something. But that one-track mind that used to demand attention isn't so important any more. I don't need the love of everybody.

Psychoanalysts Are Human, Too
By Dr. Sandor Lorand

Dr. Lorand, internationally known psychoanalyst, former president of the New York Psychoanalytic Society and of the Psychoanalytic Association of New York, of which he is now honorary president, does not consider himself a celebrity. He consented to give this brief account of his own psychoanalysis in order to clarify the question of whether the analysis a future therapist undergoes in the course of becoming a psychoanalyst differs from that of a regular patient. He makes it clear that it does not, except that the analysis of the professional is apt to be more arduous and of longer duration.

Dr. Lorand is known for educating both the public and medical colleagues in the methods of psychoanalysis. In addition to private practice and teaching activities, he has written a number of books including Technique of Psychoanalytic Therapy, Clinical Studies in Psychoanalysis *and* The Morbid Personality. *He is also founder, and director for more than ten years, of the Division of Psychoanalytic Education, State University of New York, Downstate Medical Center.*

At the end of the first World War I was working as a physician in Budapest and primarily interested in gynecology. When the short-lived Communistic government came to an end about 1920, it was followed by a reactionary period known as the Horthy regime. The Roumanians' march into Hungary resulted in oppressions of intellectuals, reactions against the democratic way of life, and restraints against Jews. So much so, that Jews were not accepted for medical or other studies at the universities. This ban also extended to hospital positions.

I left Budapest during that year because I was not allowed to retain my hospital appointment. I departed for that part of Hungary which had been ceded to Czechoslovakia after the war, a region which was one hundred percent agricultural, where I had been born and spent my childhood. The country was then being led by the famed statesman Masaryk. It was a period of enlightened democratic spirit. Physicians and intellectuals were welcomed. Living in Kosice and affiliated with the city hospital there, I had all the opportunities I needed. I worked with Dr. Jaroslaw Stuchlick, a psychiatrist who was an adherent of Jung's and who later became professor at the University of Prague.

There, in addition to my regular work, I began a research project on painless childbirth through the use of hypnosis. The results were reported in my first scientific paper. It gave me, a young physician, a certain fame to be the second doctor in Europe (a Dutch practitioner was the first) to use hypnosis to eliminate the pain of childbirth.

I had become interested in hypnosis during the first World War as a result of my work as a medical student in the Army. Although lacking a medical degree, from 1916 to 1918 I was stationed in a hospital in Budapest which received shell-shocked cases from the front. At that time the accepted treatment for these soldiers was strong electric currents (the forerunner of the electroshock therapy later brought to this country). The intention was to shock them back to health so that they could be returned to the front as quickly as possible.

But in our hospital we tried to get away from what we considered a cruel method of treating emotionally disturbed soldiers. Several of these victims had jumped out of the window after the use of the treatments. Under the chief psychiatrist's sponsorship, I started to use hypnotic suggestion and found that we obtained remarkably fast results with hypnosis.

During my last two years of medical studies I became more and more interested in psychological problems. After I settled in Czechoslovakia I wrote to Dr. Sandor Ferenczi in Budapest, author of a paper on the psycho-dynamics of hypnosis, in connection with my project on painless childbirth.

After an exchange of letters, I invited Ferenczi to give some lectures to the Medical Society of Kosice. He accepted, and in the fall of 1921, spent two days with us, lecturing to the Society as well as to a general audience.

In discussing my therapeutic work with shell-shocked soldiers during the war, and my research with painless childbirth through hypnosis, he suggested that I might try being analyzed. "Come to Budapest for six months for an analysis," he said, "You may like to do psychoanalysis. But if not, it may still be an interesting experience."

At that time psychoanalysis for doctors who wanted to enter analytic practice was both a chore and a sacrifice. Intellectually, the public was beginning to accept psychoanalysis, but paradoxically very few psychiatrists and doctors accepted it. Neurology was still in the forefront and the method of treatment for the emotional conflicts of neuroses was to give a little reassurance, or some medication, or "electric" treatment or massage, or to send patients on vacation to a "watering place" for a change of atmosphere.

If a doctor went into analysis, it meant he was interested in the emotions of his patients and the working of their minds, rather than in purely physical treatment. Such a doctor had to have a personal predilection, *a psychological attitude* for analysis. Freud described an analyst as one who was interested in the unconscious mental life, the fantasies and dreams of the patient. The doctor who became an analyst understood that when someone complained of a physical symptom, it was not necessarily organic but could be rooted in the patient's emotions.

All of the first generation, and early second generation analysts were devoted, dedicated men and women. They knew well that they were pioneering. They did not know where their patients would come from. It was as economically risky for them, as it was for Freud at the beginning of his career. In those early years analysts were individuals who were established in other fields. They came to analysis through intellectual and therapeutic interest.

The adventure inherent in Ferenczi's suggestion appealed to me. I decided to be analyzed. My chief at the hospital was willing to give me a year's leave of absence. So I went to Budapest in the Spring of 1923 and started my analysis with Ferenczi, finishing in June, 1924.

At this time, a three to six months' analysis for those training to be analysts was quite common; a nine to twelve months' analysis was considered long. Doctors, like patients, usually went six times a week. Some even went twice a day. They learned the nature of their own unconscious, as well as the hidden meanings of their dreams, the role of repression, which is the cornerstone of every neurosis, and the part played by resistance to the uncovering of what is repressed.

In the early years, most of the emphasis in analysis was on the "positive transference," the patient's feelings of love for, and dependence on the analyst, then considered the basis for therapy. But Freud soon pointed out the existence of the "negative transference," the resistance against analysis, and the feelings of unadmitted, repressed resentment against the analyst (originally against the parents) that played an important part in treatment.

In the 1920s the negative aspect of the transference relationship was fully recognized. Ferenczi led the way in emphasizing its role in the analytic process. He stressed the importance of analyzing the patient's aggressive feelings because, as he rightly said, and as Freud had said before him, frustration was one of the important elements in the creation of emotional sickness. People fall emotionally ill not because they love or are loved but because of feeling not loved or unable to love. When the baby who has felt loved feels that love decreases or ceases, he becomes frustrated and has to give up his dependency on love (a younger brother or sister may come into the family to share the love). He feels unhappy and abandoned, then he feels angry and later feels guilty about his anger.

Thus, behind his need to feel loved, a man may hide a great deal of hostility against frustrating parents. Most of us learn to repress this hostility as we grow up.

Ferenczi pointed out that "falling in love" with the analyst was easy but that it was far more difficult to be able to trust the analyst enough to express anger and resentment, hurt and shame, thus discharging emotions that arose from feelings of frustration accumulated over years of repression. This is what takes time in analysis. The patient, who is initially dependent on the analyst, learns he cannot count on him to magically make the world the way he wishes it to be, as he once did his mother and father. He has to give up this childhood dependency.

This insight, along with the greater knowledge acquired by the analyst in his own analysis as he learned how thinking, feeling, and acting are intertwined in a Gordian knot, gradually led to a longer, slower analysis. The emotional knot has to be untangled slowly as the patient's many problems are revealed. It never can be completely untangled, but the big threads can be unravelled and the smaller threads will follow.

Many a young psychiatrist goes into what is called his "training analysis" today, thinking he has come to the couch to learn about other people. Then he realizes that he has really come to be helped himself, just like everyone else. For everyone is neurotic; just becoming civilized means there will be some neurosis.

The doctor who goes through a training analysis usually finds that he is in analysis longer than the average patient. There are several reasons why. A training analysis is more difficult in that it is not only a personal, psychotherapeutic process, but also a teaching process.

In addition, the psychiatrist-in-training is apt to be someone, who, because of his intensive study of psychiatry, uses the defense of intellectuality as he faces himself. This may create more resistance against relaxation and free association than he otherwise might possess. He must also analyze the emotional content in transference, that is, what it is that takes place between him and his analyst that enables him to face himself.

Ferenczi was one of the first among Freud's associates to be analyzed by him. Ferenczi played a second only to Freud in building psychoanalysis. He is responsible for many brilliant theories and clinical contributions which Freud described as "pure gold." Very close friends, Freud called him "my dear son"; they spent many vacations together. As professor of psychoanalysis at the University of Budapest he was an inspiring teacher. He was founder and president until his death of the Hungarian Psychoanalytic Society, and for years was president of the International Psychoanalytic Association. It a source of pride to me to have been his pupil.

He, along with Jung, Ernest Jones, and A. A. Brill, accompanied Freud when he was invited to speak in 1909 at Clark University in Worcester, Massachusetts. This was the first time Freud had been invited by a university to give scientific lectures on his new discoveries—Freud himself talked about the invitation as the "realization of a daydream." Ferenczi was impressed by the interest shown in psychoanalysis and the need for an English-language journal that would bring the latest developments to the attention of English-speaking people.

In his *Collected Papers,* when Freud writes of the early history of the psychoanalytic movement and his fellow workers in other countries, he says, "Hungary has contributed only one fellow worker in psychoanalysis but S. Ferenczi outweighs a whole society."

Concerning my own history and the problems which emerged in my analysis . . . .

I was the youngest of eight children (six boys and two girls) and grew up in a very free, indulgent family. My mother was a civic leader and considered the beauty of the district where we lived. She very much wanted me to be a boy, so the story goes, since her father had just died and she wished to have a son to name after him.

My father was a gentleman farmer in a village of 500 near a city of 25,000. There were a few intellectuals in the village— my father, two other gentlemen farmers, the Catholic priest, the reform priest, the notary public (a very important man who performed marriages and kept records of births and divorces), the official who took care of roads and water supplies, and a shopkeeper.

All the peasants owned a little land of their own, but to earn a better living they also worked part-time on the large farms. We gave the land and the seeds. They planted and took care of the crops and helped with the harvesting. I remember the time of harvest as an exciting one. After the harvest was in, all the crops, except for the wheat, were shared with the peasants.

Growing up in such a community gave me a sense of freedom and love of life at an early age. I vividly remember the great fun we village children had.

Because my family was among the intellectuals, it made us feel somewhat superior. The elementary school for the children of the peasants was located in the next village, an hour's walk over the hill. The school for the children of the well-to-do was housed in a big room in one of the buildings on our farm. A schoolteacher from the city was engaged to teach the classes, usually attended by twelve to fourteen children. At the end of the year, we went to the city, about twenty-five miles away, to take the examinations. We attended this special school until we were twelve years old, then journeyed to the city for high school. In addition, our family always had a German Fraulein who taught us her native tongue.

I felt very special as the youngest child, loved by my parents, sisters, and brothers. I was the little prince, mother's darling. As a small boy, I was always taken along on her travels to the city in the horse-drawn coach, or by sleigh in winter to visit my grandparents. I was usually the only one she chose to go with her. One of my fondest memories is that of being taken out mornings when I was about three or four years old, to ride with my father in the saddle as he made his inspections of the farm. Sometimes my oldest brother, then eighteen and an overseer, would take me with him.

But I discovered later in analysis that I paid a price for this special love and attention. I became very dependent and felt very obligated to my mother and father. I needed the analyst's help to break that strong dependent-obligation, especially to my mother.

I trace my interest in becoming a physician to the early curiosity I had about people and the animals on the farm. As a child, I watched everything that went on, including the periodic visits of the bulls who impregnated the cows. I knew all about sex without ever asking a question. I played with the peasant boys and girls who were enlightened sexually and who soon enlightened me.

Although from the age of ten, I knew I wanted to be a doctor, it took me years to be able to tell my mother. She wanted me to be a philosopher and theologian, as her father had been. I was afraid to speak of my own ambitions.

My analysis showed that I was a very loyal person, in fact, that I had too much loyalty, too deep an attachment to my parents. This, in many respects, inhibited me from following my own interests. I was not ready to go against my mother's wishes until I was eighteen, and even then I could only hint at my preferences.

To please her I studied theology at the Hebrew Theological Seminary in Budapest. Even after eighteen, when I went to the University, I matriculated in philosophy and Oriental languages, studying Egyptology and the Arabic language, as well as Latin and Greek. My philosophy teacher, incidentally, was the father of the late Dr. Franz Alexander (founder of the Chicago Institute for Psychoanalysis) .

For two years I studied philosophy and languages, not daring to break away, not wanting to hurt my mother. But I "sneaked in" chemistry and physics, intending someday to transfer to medicine. I hated chemistry but knew it was required for medical school.

This was a very trying period. Having to secretly study subjects of which neither my parents nor the head of the philosophy department would have approved created considerable tension. Fortunately, no one found out. I eventually transferred to Medical School but did not tell my parents until I was drafted into the Army during the first World War. The blow was softened by the reassuring knowledge that I would be in the Medical Corps, and I was relieved of a great burden, but of course I continued to harbor guilt feelings because of the former deception.

Possessing such a deep love for my parents, not wanting to disappoint them, yet determined to follow my own interests, had created conflicts and rebellion in me. Only when I went into analysis did I discover how deep they lay. I had to be liberated from my childhood ambivalent dependence on my parents.

I always had self-confidence. The analysis augmented my self-confidence so that I did not feel too guilt-bound to my parents. The guilt stemmed from the childhood feelings, including, of course, those of the Oedipal origin. I had to realize I could go against their wishes, even leave the country as I was later to do, without feeling this would "kill" them.

As a result of problems centering around this loyalty attachment and ambivalence, I suffered the physical symptoms of stomach complaints and pains intermittently for years. They started during my military service in World War I, when I was sent back from the front. Actually this worked to my advantage in this instance for I was placed in the hospital where I worked with the shell-shocked soldiers.

After the war, the symptoms disappeared. But during analysis they were revived when my actual conflicts about future plans and dissatisfaction with the reality of Europe were causing me anxiety. As I expressed it in analysis, I felt newborn when I came out of the war alive. I wanted to start my life anew, making sure to live it fully, but I found myself caught in the conflicts over leaving my parents and leaving Europe. These conflicts brought up the symptoms once again. They were eliminated after the conflicts were resolved.

I was always optimistic, believing that wherever I was I could have a good life. In 1924 I felt that I ought to leave Europe. The little Entente (Roumania, Czechoslovakia, and Jugoslavia) mobilized against Hungary when King Karl, the former King in exile, returned to Hungary. I was drafted, this time into the Czechoslovakian Army, but spent only a few days in service, for King Karl soon left the country again and the mobilization ended.

I could have stayed, but I knew that the security was only temporary. One didn't have to be a prophet to see what was coming after World War I in Europe. My oldest brother had gone to America in 1900 to visit the Chicago Exposition and had remained there. I now decided to go, too.

My other brothers and sisters tried to persuade me to stay in Europe on the grounds that our parents were nearing seventy and that, as the only doctor in the family, my services were needed to take care of them. But I, who had always been the one most loved, now became the rebel, intent on leaving the family.

When I told Ferenczi of my intention to go to America, he wrote Dr. Brill, the leading proponent of Freudian analysis in America and the first translator of Freud into English, asking him to get me a position. Brill secured a position for me in the New York State Psychiatric Institute, then on Wards Island, and wrote Ferenczi, "We need him. Tell him to come."

During my analysis, I was in love and wanted to marry, for I always had to have a settled home. My marriage took place just prior to my departure for America. My wedding, at least, was a consolation to my parents. It was a cherished wish to see their youngest son married.

It was difficult to get visas to the United States. Many waited for years. But I was fortunate in having a position waiting for me. As a result, the American consul called and said a visa was waiting only three months after I applied. I was married in June, and sailed for the United States in August. My bride could not get a visa at once, but she joined me six months later.

When I arrived in New York, Brill was in Europe. But I was offered a position as resident at the Central Neurological Hospital on Welfare Island where I conducted the malaria treatment. In September of that year, I met some of the analysts who had come to Vienna during 1922 and 1923 to be analyzed by Freud. They knew Ferenczi who had traveled to Vienna on weekends to lecture to them.

In the Fall of 1927, I was invited by Dr. Israel Strauss, chief of the Neuropsychiatric Division of Mt. Sinai Hospital in New York, to join the Mental Health Clinic of the hospital. There I took part in both teaching and therapy and I also undertook postgraduate teaching of psychiatrists at Columbia University's Medical School, College of Physicians and Surgeons. For the past thirty-five years, I have been active in teaching, as well as in private practice.

My analysis had enabled me to leave my parents and journey without guilt to America, the second European psychoanalyst to do so. Otto Rank, a student of Freud's, who later broke away from Freud, was the first. There was only a handful of analysts in America at the time I arrived.

I have always believed analysts should have a love of life apart from their scientific interest. Their love should not merely be restricted to their work. My childhood play and enjoyment of all kinds of sports and games carried through my later life. Our farm was by the side of a big river which meant swimming and fishing in summer and skating in winter. We also had plenty of opportunity for horseback riding and sleigh riding.

As a university student, I continued to ride horseback, and added figure-skating to the list of sports I enjoyed. In my medical years, I became especially fond of fencing, and in my analytic years, my sparring partner in saber-fencing was Geza Roheim, the anthropologist, a first-class fencer. We continued our fencing bouts in America after he came here. Incidentally, I formed the first fencing group at the YMHA in New York in the early 1930s, teaching fencing in the building at Lexington Avenue and 92nd Street.

I continued figure-skating up until a few years ago. Ernest Jones, also a figure-skater, wrote in addition to his psychoanalytic books, a volume entitled *The Elements of Figure Skating,* of which he said he was very proud. He inscribed a copy for my wife and me: "To my dear friends Sandor and Rhoda Lorand, For the edification of the one and the instruction of the other. With kindest regards, Ernest Jones."

Rhoda is my second wife, whom I married a year after the death of my first. She is a psychoanalyst specializing in the treatment of children and adolescents, and author of the recent book, *Love, Sex and the Teenager.* She edits my papers and books and psychoanalyzes me in her spare time. From time to time she can be heard to say that I am a false advertisement for psychoanalysis and that I could use a little anxiety. She says, "People think it's your analysis that has made you so unself-conscious, optimistic, and confident—and so free of animosity — whereas, if the truth be told, it is the result of having been the darling of the family and the favorite of both parents." Freud did say that being mother's favorite child gives one a feeling of invincibility. I feel that it has been true in my case. Nothing keeps me down and I manage to land on my feet from whatever blows fate deals me.

My greatest interest has been treating and healing patients, but equally important has been spreading the knowledge of psychoanalysis to the medical profession and to the public. In common with all the pioneers, I have felt it part of my task to bring about recognition of psychoanalysis, and have worked toward that end from the moment I arrived in America.

In 1948 this conviction led me to organize the Division of Psychoanalytic Education of the State University of New York, Downstate Medical Center, on the invitation of Dr. Howard Potter, the chairman of the psychiatric department. I was the first director of this official training institute for psychoanalyts, which includes a free psychoanalytic clinic where patients are analyzed four times a week without fee.

This was Freud's dream—to have psychoanalysis taught in universities and medical schools. But the most he was able to do in the hostile city of Vienna, where he had aroused the wrath of the medical profession, was to become a lecturer at the University of Vienna. Ferenczi became the world's first full professor of psychoanalysis, in Budapest.

I have visited Hungary twice since coming to America; first in 1929, when both parents were alive, and again in 1931, after my father died. My mother died before World War II and was thus spared the horrors of the Hitler regime. By then, all my family, except for my oldest sister and a brother, had come to America. Those two remained in Hungary and died in a concentration camp with part of their family (some had managed to escape).

When I first informed my parents that I was going to leave Europe, live in America, and practice psychoanalysis there, my father said, "If you want to go, it's your life."

My mother was heartbroken but gave me her blessing.

The last time I saw them both together, in 1929, I realized that finally I was visiting them not out of guilt, but out of love. This was what my analysis had done for me. I had achieved a freedom from guilt which allowed me to decide to leave, knowing there had to be a gratification of selfish interests if those interests were ones which could be ethically and morally substantiated, even though my act might hurt dear ones.

During my last visit in 1931, I brought my mother a copy of my first book, *The Morbid Personality,* which had just been published by Knopf. She was very proud and I am sure that she forgave me for leaving her, knowing that the independent spirit is the only free spirit.

No More "Shoulds"
By Vivian Vance

Miss Vance is known to America's television viewers from "I Love Lucy" and "The Lucy Show" on which she appeared for foureen years. She is married to John Dodds, a publishing executive, and frequently appears in plays and on various TV shows.

What a wonderful feeling it is to wake up every morning and face the day with joy, knowing that you're going to do the best you can, instead of allowing life to stampede you. You accept the day with its joys and sorrows, instead of feeling depressed and despairing.

That's what analysis did for me. My experience on the couch and since has been the greatest thing that ever happened to me. I have gone through a lot of heartache to find out what I really want in life, and with the help of analysis, I finally know.

A new well of vitality has burst within me and has never run dry. Analysis gave me a great release of energy. Some people fear analysis because they feel it will diminish their talent.

They believe their neurosis is making them talented. I can only speak for myself, but analysis made me more aware of my resources. Only now I don't care about the work so desperately. I work for joy, and for the money—it's sort of like going to the store.

The neurosis doesn't rule me any more. I used to apologize for my constant fatigue, working so hard to make good, trying so hard to get everyone's approval. Now I only care about my own approval.

I also found out, thanks to analysis, that neurosis frequently drives one to pick the wrong mate. Much to my sorrow, this was true of my marriage to my ex-husband.

When you marry neurotically, your least desirable qualities emerge. All your hostile projections rise up to clash with those of your partner. The anger and feelings of ambivalence stem from childhood and relate to your attitudes toward your parents. When you marry neurotically, you marry someone like your parents, wanting their approval just as you wanted the approval of your parents. You are constantly living for someone else's actions and reactions rather than living out your own life. One of the great joys today comes from my having been able to choose to be married to an entirely different type of man.

Even today, eight years after the analysis ended (I went twice, because the first time I left much too early—like graduating from high school when you are in the fourth grade), there is still the thrill of discovery. "Is *that* why I did that?" I still say every so often when I get a new insight.

I went into the analysis knowing I wanted to change so perhaps that put me ahead of the game. I had two lists—one describing my reactions as they were at the time, the second, listing the way I would like to be.

For instance, I wanted to know why I threw up if I heard a dirty word, or why I was afraid to fly. I wanted to be able to stand hearing dirty words, and to fly without fear.

There is so much to understand about inner conflicts. At first, it's shocking to face your secret self. It's difficult, but so worth the struggle. I wanted so much to understand *why*.

For years, I played the comedienne onstage, but my life off-stage was anything but fun. I felt deeply depressed, and the depression finally erupted in the late 1940s when I was struggling to make it on Broadway. Although I kept propelling myself toward stardom, I felt that there was another, more genuine kind of life that I was missing. I was the life of the party, and a great cook. I gave away anything I owned to anyone who admired it. I wanted to please everyone at any cost to myself. Above all, I had to feel people liked me.

It was too much, and I paid for the waste of energy by becoming physically and emotionally ill. I suffered from arthritis and other ailments, and went in and out of doctors' offices like a sick morning glory. When I think of the money I spent on specialists, all of whom agreed I was ill! Now, after analysis, every pain, every ache, has disappeared.

During the early 1950s, I fought to get possession of myself again, as we started the *I Love Lucy* show. After several years of analysis, I knew I had changed. It was during this time that I divorced and remarried. I didn't have to be on the go all the time. I enjoyed quiet things, such as sitting at home with John reading a book, or buying things for the house that gave us both pleasure.

I now can look at the world outside me, no longer involved with my own desperation. I have tried to explain to others how they, too, can be helped if they feel emotionally troubled.

My interest in helping others started when I appeared as the guest star on *Candid Camera.* I stood behind the lingerie counter of a Los Angeles department store, with the camera trained on the customers' reactions to me as "saleslady."

A young man walked over to buy a nightgown. I asked, "Who is it for?"

Tears came into his eyes. He told me he was buying the nightgown for his wife who was in a mental hospital. I called out to the cameraman to cut off the camera. I wanted only to help the young man, not to make a spectacle of him. I asked if his wife would like to talk to somebody who also had been emotionally ill and who had become well. He was overjoyed at my interest.

I went to the hospital and saw her, and found I was good at reassuring others. When we lived in Connecticut, I became co-chairman of "Operation Friendship," a project to recruit volunteers for the Connecticut Association for Mental Health. I spoke all over the state, visited mental hospitals, talked with patients, answered their questions. I also worked with teen-agers at the High Meadows Treatment Center where young boys received help.

I was so pleased when, at one hospital, a woman who had not spoken for years started to talk to me. They told me later that she was soon well enough to be discharged. A psychiatrist at the Norwich Hospital once said to me, "Because you talk so freely about your own illness and recovery, you get across the idea that others can he helped, too. You give them the feeling that people on the outside, celebrities like you, are concerned about them, and they immediately feel much better."

I also have written to a number of men and women I met, sometimes sending postcards when I have a spare moment. I don't call my work "charity." I do what I do simply because I want to, because I get satisfaction out of it. We all want to be loving and to give to others. It just takes some of us longer to understand ourselves so we are able to give love.

My analysis is over now, and as Martha Scott, one of my best friends, said to me, "You are the happiest woman I know."

I feel happy—not silly-happy, but with the happiness that comes from being a contented, fulfilled woman. I wish that all the men and women who have problems could afford the treatment which has brought me such joy.

Creative Release
By Richard Florsheim

Mr. Florsheim, internationally known painter and print-maker, is represented in some fifty museums throughout the world, including the Metropolitan Museum of Art, the Museum of Modern Art, the New York Public Library, the Art Institute of Chicago, the Smithsonian Institute, and the Library of Congress. He is a member of the Illinois Arts Council, an honorary vice-president of the Provincetown Art Association, and an honorary president of Artists Equity Association.

I could write a book about my analysis, so the question is not what to include but what to leave out. Every aspect of my life is involved. Some of it I do not want to put in print, for it is my concern alone. Other aspects I cannot write about because I have no words for the feelings involved.

So, when I write of my analysis, I must, of necessity, do it on an incomplete level. I feel that the heart of the matter is my own business and I would no more write of the deepest levels than walk down the street naked. The very reason for going into analysis is to be able to communicate aspects of personality that, under other circumstances, cannot be discussed, to admit to yourself such feelings as shame, guilt, fear. It takes a long time to face them, even in treatment.

I had heard little of psychoanalysis before the war. Stationed in Washington by the Navy, I roomed in the house of a friend. She must have been aware of the conflicts going on inside of me, aware of my hostilities, even though I was not, for she started to leave articles about psychoanalysis around the house. I am like a vacuum cleaner about printed matter; I pick up anything around and read it. So I read the articles about psychoanalysis. I started to think, "That might be me," and "Maybe analysis would help." I spoke to my friend about it and asked her if she thought I needed analysis. She said, gently, that she believed I would benefit greatly from the experience.

I approached treatment as I do everything, with a great deal of intensity. After being discharged from the Navy, I immediately drove almost nonstop to Chicago and the Institute for Psychoanalysis. I had my separation pay and this helped me get started.

Before I entered the Navy, I had a hard time establishing my own identity. My mother died when I was sixteen and my father, a businessman *(not* the Florsheim of the shoe company), brought up my older brother and myself. I wanted to be an artist but he objected. It is hard enough to become an artist *with* help. Opposition makes it even more difficult. There was no malice on his part in opposing my choice; he had real fears for me and the problems he sensed I would have to face.

I knew I would be confronted by the same conflicts on returning to Chicago. I thought that analysis might help me to find a solution.

I went into analysis with a chip on my shoulder, afraid, as are many artists, that it would destroy my creative drive. I told the analyst this. She said, "If you are really creative, you will emerge from treatment even more so. If you are not really creative, is it not better to find it out now, while you are young?"

I wanted to get through my analysis as quickly as possible so that I could devote all my energies to painting. But, as everyone who has been in it knows, it cannot be rushed. For the next two years I went five times a week, sometimes six and even seven. I even importuned the doctor to see me at home on Sundays.

At the beginning, I felt that my analyst had to see my working environment, my studio in the basement of my father's house in the suburbs, and my paintings in order to understand me. I urged her to come out and look at my work. She finally did so, politely and noncommittally. After seeing my work, she said, "Now, let's get on to the analysis."

"I wanted you to see the paintings, so that you could understand me," I protested.

"I am an analyst—not an art critic," she said. "I am analyzing you, not your work."

This was the beginning of the end of painting of such compulsive, autobiographical pictures. Though it took many years for the change to take place, my fantasy that I could only be approached through my work began to disappear. Anyone who knows the evolution of my style can see the difference. Every artist's style changes over the years. That is part of the process of creative growth. But the deep change—of my point of departure—was triggered by analysis.

At the time I started treatment, I was completely unknown; I had no dealer, no teaching position. What money I had went for the daily sessions. I was lucky to get gas for the car for the daily twenty-five-mile drive to the Institute.

My father would not help me financially. He was determined that I make it on my own. Though I did not realize it at the time it was the best thing he could have done. He was wise and strong enough to withhold his financial support, though it must have been difficult for him not to indulge me. He wanted me to take the consequences of my own decisions. I hated him for it at the time; I thought him selfish and cruel. Fortunately, he lived many years, long enough so that we enjoyed years of friendship before he died. I had many opportunities to express my appreciation to him and he took great pleasure in my later professional recognition. Thanks to him I have had the satisfaction of knowing that I have fought my own battles (and even won some of them) without the cushion of money.

I dove into analysis with everything I had. For me, it was like reaching for a life preserver miraculously encountered in an endless ocean. It was a matter of life or death, of basic survival.

It was brief, twenty-two months in all. I have never gone back nor had a "return engagement." I knew from the beginning what I wanted and, as soon as I had an even tenuous grasp on it, I wanted to live and produce. Treatment was broken off abruptly, with the full understanding on my part that it was not finished. I think analysis never really finishes, neatly and cleanly. Life itself is not neat and clean. There are many paradoxes and contradictions in life and in analysis, as part of that life. I feel sure that if I ever find myself in another emotional cul-de-sac, I will be perfectly willing to go back into treatment. I left college after a year and a half because my interests and aspirations were elsewhere at the time. But, if it becomes necessary to go back and get a degree, I would not hesitate. I feel the same way about analysis.

A great deal of what I have done would have been much more difficult without analysis, but I think I would have done it anyway. I believe it would have been a greater struggle and would have taken much longer. You get out of treatment what you bring to it. I had a tremendous need for reassurance and an understanding of the roadblocks in my life. I needed to find out why they were blocks and who put them in my way. I discovered it was myself, of course.

Partly because of the early resistance of my family to my being an artist and their disapproval, I had a tremendous drive for "success." After analysis, I began to realize that the practice of my art is in itself the satisfaction, not the rewards emanating from it. Perhaps, without help, I would never have come to accept this. As I began to realize that I was probably not a genius, that I certainly was not one at the moment and very likely would never be one, I started to relax and be happy. I could derive my satisfactions from the work itself. And, as a result, my work began to flow, improve, and change. Such an inner realization is not easy in a success-oriented society, where the deeper values of the artist can become submerged and overwhelmed by the competitive stresses of our time.

I know many artists who are plagued by jealousies; this

seems almost symptomatic of the creative professions. One reason may be that some of us must keep proving that we are not as inadequate creatively as we fear we are. Analysis helped to reduce this fear, and today I have more of a sense of my own worth as a human being, not just for what I can produce. Life is much happier as a result.

Of course there are regrets about the analysis. I sometimes think, "Perhaps I could have gone deeper." But analysis is a very imperfect, very partial process, as are most of life's experiences. Many of us expect a complete answer; we want miracles, magic. But treatment is not magic and does not provide complete answers. It is not as simple as a bad tooth which can have the decay removed and the space filled with gold. It is not a matter of black or white, good or bad, troubled or serene.

Attempting to look back and remember what happened is like any glance backward on a life experience—I tend to remember the good and not the painful. A surgeon once told me that even the most agonizing pain is soon forgotten by the patient. This is a kind of protection; there is a blurring of the pain. I remember certain highlights and critical turning points, but details now escape me. Yet I do remember that it was exceedingly painful at times. There were moments akin to having my appendix removed without an anesthetic.

There were other times when I felt it to be a waste of time, even a fake. At other moments I was so involved that I believed that *everyone* should be analyzed.

I am a volcano inside. I can change very quickly from happiness to depression, from inspiration to discouragement. As a result of analysis, I can know that I *am* that way and accept it without worry. This serene exterior which covers the inner tumultuousness *is* my nature and not a catastrophe that must be feared and denied.

When I first went to the Institute, I was terrified that someone would see me going into the place. I felt that what I was talking about behind that closed door somehow would show on my face in the waiting room. I even felt that it would be a disaster if acquaintances guessed that I was in treatment. How differently I feel today, as I sit at my desk and write these words for publication.

In the stirred-up state of mind in which I began, I was frightened of analysis. Today I accept it as part of my education, or my war experiences, or my failures and successes. "Man does not live by bread alone"—nor does he live by analysis alone. Though it is one of the larger experiences of my life, it is only one of them. Those who must keep talking about their experiences in analysis are not really through with it.

Perhaps some of the more esoteric manifestations of contemporary art could not be done by people who had had the experience of analysis. They would not, perhaps, be so interested in attracting attention to themselves. It is equally possible that those who sometimes express admiration for such works might have less need to do so if they had more insight into themselves.

There are many artists who are constantly running away to remote places. It seems to me that they are often trying to run away from themselves. I think I learned not to run away from myself. People often ask me why I continue to live in Chicago. I stay here for the same reason that Nelson Algren does. It is real to me. I love it; I hate it; I have an equation with it. And it understands me. I feel I have a meaning here that I do not have in any other place. Though I am not here very much of the year, for we have a summer home in Provincetown and I have to make frequent trips to Europe, Chicago is home base, an anchor, a reality. With all its faults, I can identify with it. And I think that this, too, is a part of the resuls of analysis, acceping where I am in time and place and being able to cope with it.

I cannot say too strongly that I feel analysis is no panacea. It provides no final resolution of conflicts. What it does is to remove some of the short circuits so that you do not go on blowing so many fuses. It does not turn you into a smoothly functioning computer, but you are less accident-prone on an emotional level. Even the most perfect machines sometimes blow fuses and the most beautifully analyzed people get depressed, unhappy, or confused, on occasion.

Nor do I wish to convey the impression that I think I know all the answers. One thing I surely learned was that it is all right to accept a multiplicity of levels, all right not to make sweeping judgments or absolute dividing lines. I no longer feel the need to say "This is absolutely a good painting" or "This is absolutely bad." I know better how to live with flux and flow and uncertainty.

A poet once said about my paintings, "I like them because they have so many different meanings." I have always remembered these words, for I feel that we do violence to any experience, any painting, any relatedness in saying, "This is *absolutely* right or wrong, good or bad." I think it was Anatole France who said that, "Absolutes in ideas lead to fanaticisms in action."

My early paintings were autobiographical. Slowly, with the help of analysis, I have gained, and hope I am still gaining, more insight into the world about me. I can now more readily let it come to me, rather than attack it.

Analysis helped me to realize how much of my energy was used up in fighting unresolved battles, in running around in a circle trying to catch my own tail. I do not think that it lessened my artistic productivity. It increased it and changed its focus. My creative drive was released, not destroyed.

The Revolver in the Corner Cupboard
By Graham Greene

The prolific and esteemed author of many novels including
The Heart of the Matter, The Quiet American, the Comedi-
ans, The Third Man, *plays, short stories, and essays, Greene di-
vides his fiction into two groups—entertainment and moral
seriousness, the latter probing such matters as sin and the nature of faith. Nearly all his fiction has been highly successful,
and nearly all the books have been excitingly filmed.*

I can remember very clearly the afternoon I found the revolver in the brown deal corner cupboard in the bedroom
which I shared with my elder brother. It was the early autumn
of 1922. I was seventeen and terribly bored and in love with
my sister's governess—one of those miserable, hopeless, romantic loves of adolescence that set in many minds the idea
that love and despair are inextricable and that successful love
hardly deserves the name. At that age one may fall irrevocably
in love with failure, and success of any kind loses its savour

before it is experienced. Such a love is surrendered once and for all to the singer at the pavement's edge, the bankrupt, the old school friend who wants to touch you for a dollar. Perhaps in many so conditioned it is the love for God that mainly survives, because in his eyes they can imagine themselves remaining always drab, seedy, unsuccessful, and therefore worthy of notice.

The revolver was a small genteel object with six chambers like a tiny egg stand, and there was a cardboard box of bullets. It has only recently occurred to me that they may have been blanks; I always assumed them to be live ammunition, and I never mentioned the discovery to my brother because I had realized the moment I saw the revolver the use I intended to make of it. (I don't to this day know why he possessed it; certainly he had no license, and he was only three years older than myself. A large family is as departmental as a Ministry.)

My brother was away—probably climbing in the Lake District—and until he returned the revolver was to all intents mine. I knew what to do with it because I had been reading a book (the name Ossendowski comes to mind as the possible author) describing how the White Russian officers, condemned to inaction in South Russia at the tail-end of the counter-revolutionary war, used to invent hazards with which to escape boredom. One man would slip a charge into a revolver and turn the chambers at random, and his companion would put the revolver to his head and pull the trigger. The chance, of course, was six to one in favour of life.

How easily one forgets emotions. If I were dealing now with an imaginary character, I would feel it necessary for verisimilitude to make him hesitate, put the revolver back into the cupboard, return to it again after an interval, reluctantly and fear-fully, when the burden of boredom became too great. But in fact I think there was no hesitation at all, for the next I can remember is crossing Berkhamsted Common, gashed here and there between the gorse bushes with the stray trenches of the first Great War, towards the Ashridge beeches. Perhaps before I had made the discovery, boredom had already reached an in-tolerable depth.

I think the boredom was far deeper than the love. It had al-ways been a feature of childhood: it would set in on the second day of the school holidays. The first day was all happiness, and, after the horrible confinement and publicity of school, seemed to consist of light, space and silence. But a prison conditions its inhabitants. I never wanted to return to it (and finally ex-pressed my rebellion by the simple act of running away), but yet I was so conditioned that freedom bored me unutterably.

The psychoanalysis that followed my act of rebellion had fixed the boredom as hypo fixes the image on the negative. I emerged from those delightful months in London spent at my analyst's house—perhaps the happiest months of my life—cor-rectly orientated, able to take a proper extrovert interest in my fellows (the jargon rises to the lips), but wrung dry. For years, it seems to me, I could take no aesthetic interest in any visual thing at all: staring at a sight that others assured me was beau-tiful, I would feel nothing. I was fixed in my boredom. (Writ-ing this I come on a remark of Rilke: "Psychoanalysis is too fundamental a help for me, it helps you once and for all, it clears you up, and to find myself finally cleared up one day might be even more helpless than this chaos.")

Now with the revolver in my pocket I was beginning to

emerge. I had stumbled on the perfect cure. I was going to escape in one way or another, and because escape was inseparably connected with the Common in my mind, it was there that I went.

The wilderness of gorse, old trenches, abandoned butts was the unchanging backcloth of most of the adventures of childhood. It was to the Common I had decamped for my act of rebellion some years before, with the intention, expressed in a letter left after breakfast on the heavy black sideboard, that there I would stay, day and night, until either I had starved or my parents had given in; when I pictured war it was always in terms of this Common, and myself leading a guerilla campaign in the ragged waste, for no one, I was persuaded, knew its paths so intimately (how humiliating that in my own domestic campaign I was ambushed by my elder sister after a few hours).

Beyond the Common lay a wide grass ride known for some reason as Cold Harbour to which I would occasionally with some fear take a horse, and beyond this again stretched Ashridge Park, the smooth olive skin of beech trees and the thick last year's quagmire of leaves, dark like old pennies. Deliberately I chose my ground, I believe without any real fear—perhaps because I was uncertain myself whether I was play-acting; perhaps because so many acts which my elders would have regarded as neurotic, but which I still consider to have been under the circumstances highly reasonable, lay in the background of this more dangerous venture.

There had been, for example, perhaps five or six years before, the disappointing morning in the dark room by the linen cupboard on the eve of term when I had patiently drunk a quantity of hypo under the impression that it was poisonous: on another occasion the blue glass bottle of hay fever lotion which as it contained a small quantity of cocaine had probably been good for my mood: the bunch of deadly nightshade that I had eaten with only a slight narcotic effect: the twenty aspirins I had taken before swimming in the empty out-of-term school baths (I can still remember the curious sensation of swimming through wool): these acts may have removed all sense of strangeness as I slipped a bullet into a chamber and, holding the revolver behind my back, spun the chambers round.

Had I romantic thoughts about the governess? Undoubtedly I must have had, but I think that at the most they simply eased the medicine down. Boredom, aridity, those were the main emotions. Unhappy love has, I suppose, sometimes driven boys to suicide, but this was not suicide, whatever a coroner's jury might have said of it: it was a gamble with six chances to one against an inquest. The romantic flavor—the autumn scene, the small heavy compact shape lying in the fingers—that perhaps was a tribute to adolescent love, but the discovery that it was possible to enjoy again the visible world by risking its total loss was one I was bound to make sooner or later.

I put the muzzle of the revolver in my right ear and pulled the trigger. There was a minute click, and looking down at the chamber I could see that the charge had moved into place. I was out by one. I remember an extraordinary sense of jubilation. It was as if a light had been turned on. My heart was knocking in its cage, and I felt that life contained an infinite number of possibilities. It was like a young man's first successful experience of sex—as if in that Ashridge glade one had passed a test of manhood. I went home and put the revolver back in the corner cupboard.

The odd thing about this experience was that it was repeated several times. At fairly long intervals I found myself craving for the drug. I took the revolver with me when I went up to Oxford and I would walk out from Headington towards Elsfield down what is now a wide arterial road, smooth and shiny like the walls of a public lavatory. Then it was a sodden unfrequented country lane. The revolver would be whipped behind my back, the chambers twisted, the muzzle quickly and surreptitiously inserted beneath the black and ugly winter tree, the trigger pulled.

Slowly the effect of the drug wore off—I lost the sense of jubilation, I began to gain from the experience only the crude kick of excitement. It was like the difference between love and lust. And as the quality of the experience deteriorated so my sense of responsibility grew and worried me. I wrote a very bad piece of free verse (free because it was easier in that way to express my meaning without literary equivocation) describing how, in order to give a fictitious sense of danger, I would "press the trigger of a revolver I already know to be empty." This piece of verse I would leave permanently on my desk, so that if I lost my gamble, there would be incontrovertible evidence of an accident, and my parents, I thought, would be less troubled than by an apparent suicide—or than by the rather bizarre truth.

But it was back at Berkhamsted that I paid a permanent farewell to the drug. As I took my fifth dose it occurred to me that I wasn't even excited: I was beginning to pull the trigger about as casually as I might take an aspirin tablet. I decided to give the revolver—which was six-chambered—a sixth and last chance. Twirling the chambers round, I put the muzzle to my ear for the last time and heard the familiar empty click as the chambers revolved. I was through with the drug, and walking back over the Common, down the new road by the ruined castle, past the private entrance to the gritty old railway station —reserved for the use of Lord Brownlow—my mind was already busy on other plans. One campaign was over, but the war against boredom had got to go on.

I put the revolver back in the corner cupboard, and going downstairs I lied gently and convincingly to my parents that a friend had invited me to join him in Paris.

What I Meant to Tell My Analyst
By Eddie Jaffe

Publicity as we know it today is indebted to Eddie Jaffe for many of its techniques. His accounts have included the governments of Indonesia and Iceland, the U.S. Treasury Law Enforcement Agencies, U.S. Steel, Singer Co., Cinerama, TV networks and motion picture companies. He has also represented a long list of personalities as varied as Jackie Gleason, Joe E. Lewis, Joe Namath, Huntington Hartford and Rocky Graziano. He is credited with having encouraged former Governor Jimmy Davis of Louisiana, then a singer, to run for office. He created the hit show, This Was Burlesque, *and is now pioneering in CATV programming.*

Mr. Jaffe has also lectured at universities on the relationship between psychoanalysis and public relations and was a founder of the Association for Applied Psychoanalysis.

I first discovered Freud at the age of fourteen when I was living in an orphan home in Cleveland, Ohio (I was there for three years until the age of sixteen). The assistant superintendent of the home, Jack Girick, was in analysis at the time, and his psychoanalytic understanding helped many of us over rough spots.

Having this favorable indoctrination to psychoanalysis, I don't understand why it took sixteen painful years before I sought the help that was so readily available. For nearly a quarter of a century previously, I visited doctors in dozens of cities because of digestive problems. My symptoms had been given many names, and even more remedies, none of which worked. I was even hospitalized with gastroenteritis, but no one hinted a possible emotional origin.

That is, not until I became a patient of Dr. Cyril Solomon, whose clientele regard themselves as the most "in" club of our time. I had developed an illness that was almost completely incapacitating. After examining me he said, "I can treat the symptoms, but not what's causing them. I know a psychiatrist who might be able to help you, if you want to try."

"You think I'm nuts?" I asked. I shared the popular impression that visiting a psychiatrist was putting your foot into the door of an insane asylum.

"Not at all," he said. "Many of our physical problems are tied in with emotions."

He recommended me to an outstanding psychoanalyst who was a member of the New York Psychoanalytic Institute, the most Freudian of all Institutes in this country, if not the world. Its members have been called the "guardians" of Freudian analysis, as opposed to some groups which the Freudians feel "distil" or "distort" psychoanalysis.

The analyst lived on Central Park South. The first problem we discussed was why I couldn't afford to pay his fee. This is the first problem with which all analysts deal and it must be successfully solved if the analysis is not to end immediately. I think of the story of the analyst who told the patient, "The payments are fifty dollars a visit, five times a week." The patient answered, "Okay, Doctor, that solves your problem— now what about mine?"

But far more humorous than this story is the oft-heard assertion that people go into analysis because it is "fashionable." I've never known anyone who would endure the pain and public exposure of his secret self in order to "belong." A sadistic dentist who drilled teeth without anesthesia would be equally painful and far less expensive and time-consuming.

The road to any psychoanalyst's office is paved with desperation.

The possibility of my developing a warm relationship with my psychoanalyst was difficult since in appearance and personality he reminded me of Governor Thomas E. Dewey. I also recall his opening remark to me, "You're the unhappiest looking person I've ever met." He may have been completely accurate in his estimation of my personality, but this did not endear him to me, nor did it help put me at ease in this new and strange experience.

During the four years that I went to him five times a week our relationship didn't improve very much. One reason was my feeling that he regarded the work I did as frivolous and unimportant. I didn't so much resent the fact that he called my work *"frou frou,"* as that he used a word I couldn't understand, and the translation of which varies. I learned later, he had been an orthodox or right-wing Communist, and I felt as though I were being analyzed by Stalin.

In its early years, my analysis was far more helpful to my friends than it was to me. The patient in analysis often plays doctor and projects the intellectual insight he acquires on his friends and business acquaintances. I built up one of the largest unfrocked psychoanalytic practices in the midtown New York area. I realize now that I should have saved these emotions for my own analysis, but then I was too dedicated a psychoanalytic convert not to pass on its benefits. One of the recipients was the editor of this book who, at the time, worked down the street as a reporter for *The New York Times* and later wrote a book about her analysis.

Incidentally, it is, I am sure, the ambition of every patient who works in the field of communications to someday write about his analysis. But I have the same problem in recalling the day-to-day events of the analysis that I do in many other areas of my life. I envy those who kept notes and later wrote books about their experience on the couch, although some psychoanalysts say that if a patient has to write a book about his analysis, he needs more analysis. P. S.: This does not apply to the editor of this book.

Because of the talking I did about my own analysis, I would safely say there are dozens of people who went to psychiatrists and psychologists far earlier than they might have otherwise. But, as I said, I could have got much more out of my own analysis and saved hundreds of dollars, not to mention hours, if I hadn't made such effective use of my intellectuality, one of the classical defenses against the painful truth acquired in the analyst's office.

Another favorite defense was the "Not me—you, doctor" reaction. It is so easy to believe that the analyst's interpretation applies more to himself than to you. Often I refused to admit that he was the doctor and I was the patient.

Still another of my defenses was the demand for magic. I went to the analyst so he would "cure" me. I wanted him to write a prescription, as though I had the flu or a stomachache. I wanted him to explain me to myself, or to give me one of the "instant cures" so readily available in popular literature. It was not until I started to accept the fact that I had to cure myself that I began to make progress.

Now when I become impatient with people whose self-destructiveness is readily apparent, I have to consciously say to myself, "There is no magic. Neither hypnosis, truth serum, tranquilizer, electroshock, nor rest and relaxation, shall clear away the snow, rain, heat, or gloom of the mind that keeps us prisoners of our emotions."

It is difficult twenty years later to remember many details about my analysis. But one remark made by the analyst has troubled me ever since. Some time before I terminated treatment he said, "You've crossed the Rubicon. I didn't think you would make it."

During the four years with him, I often wondered whether my resistance to achieving a positive transference (a warm relationship with the analyst much as you "loved" your mother and father) was not due to my own unique point of view and problems, for my analyst is one of the most respected men in his field, elected to some of the highest offices in the country by his colleagues. I am sure he is regarded by some of his patients as a most kindly, warm figure (although the only other one of his patients whom I know had exactly the same reaction to him that I did).

Another incident that led me to wonder about some of his interpretations occurred when I was hospitalized for virus pneumonia. The diagnosis of the illness was confirmed by X-rays. My analyst had, in the beginning, insisted it was purely an emotional upset. But Dr. Solomon, who whisked me into the hospital, refused to doubt the verdict of his X-ray plates. He called my analyst to talk about my physical symptoms with him.

My analyst said, "I'm sorry, but I can't discuss my patient with you."

Dr. Solomon was somewhat taken aback, inasmuch as he thought I was *his* patient, sent by him to the analyst.

One of my main difficulties in analysis was almost a complete amnesia about my childhood prior to age six. (I have since learned that Freud said this was true of almost everyone; he termed it "childhood amnesia.") But it troubled me to such an extent that I made a special trip back to Duluth and Hibbing, Minnesota, where I was born and lived as an infant.

However, I could find no one who could remember or tell me any of the events leading to the death of my mother some twenty-eight years previously. After she died, when I was six, my father had sent me to live with relatives in a nearby village before I finally wound up at the orphans' home.

I was giving up and returning to New York when, because I had a few hours to spare between trains in Duluth, I decided to visit a distant relative with whom I had sometimes spent summer vacations. When she overheard me discussing my frustrated search for my past with her daughter, she broke in to say, "I didn't want to tell you this but—" She went on to describe a family situation that confirmed many of my analyst's interpretations and accounted for many of my deeper feelings.

During analysis I realized the strength of the emotions which can sweep through you after a session with the analyst. It is incomprehensible to anyone who has never experienced it. The anger you finally allow yourself to feel is most difficult to control. It is a happy day for those close to you when you finally begin to understand how you have displaced your rage from those who originally caused it, to others on whom it is safe to vent it.

When I reached what my analyst described as a "plateau," we mutually decided to end the analysis. The "plateau" meant that I was willing to give up certain "symptoms" but refused to change what analysts describe as "character traits." The definition of a symptom is something which both you and the analyst agree is harmful to you. A character trait is something which the analyst thinks is either destructive to you or not in keeping with what he regards as the person you should be.

We come here to what I believe is the basic issue of any form of therapy—its purpose. I know a Marxian analyst who thought he'd cured a patient when the latter gave up a $50,000 a year job in which the analyst felt he "exploited" others, and took a $10,000 a year job which the analyst believed was more socially useful. There are also analysts who impose their standards of morality on a patient without allowing the patient his own standards. There are those like my analyst, who are judgmental about the value of a patient's profession, feeling it is "beneath" him because it would be "beneath" them. These analysts sound more like teachers, ministers, or rabbis, and sometimes seem to forget that their primary purpose is to join the patient in the exploration of his unconscious.

During the four years of my analysis my income increased, but I still lived in a world which, in my analyst's words, I "had created," not the world of "reality." What I had done, he said, was to people my world with rejected, odd, offbeat, antisocial characters. Thus I managed to live in a world that was both my fantasy and my reality. One of the most helpful things I achieved was the understanding that you see what you want to see. If you want to regard the world as full of hostile, vengeful persons it is easy enough to find them.

About two years after I discontinued analysis I again sought professional help, since I was still suffering from physical symptoms. I selected Dr. Aaron Karush, a psychiatrist who was associated with Columbia University Medical School and who had done experimental work with patients with intestinal disorders, observing the role emotions played on the digestive process.

My relationship with him became one of discussing day-to-day problems when they arose. I saw him on the average of once a week or less, but I went for five years. There was no couch; we talked face-to-face. This is a form of treatment known as psychotherapy. In my case it was far more rewarding than my analysis.

I am sure my analysis was incomplete. I will never know what the results might have been had I, or my analyst, succeeded in going further in the conventional Freudian analysis.

What made it incomplete was my refusal to admit defeat. I was too stubborn to face up to the fact that I was not changing, and that perhaps I was not using as many of the analyst's interpretations to understand myself as I might have.

The great moments of analysis come as you realize the truth about yourself—it is as though an electric light has been turned on in a dark room. At such a time you think, "My God, this is so apparent. Why didn't I realize it before?"

Even after analysis, it was hard to understand the weeks, months, and years of reaching through levels and levels of unconscious feeling before you finally see so clearly the emotional background of your decisions.

Sometimes those who have the greatest need for emotional help say to you, "Why do I need somebody else to tell me about myself?" The more help a person needs, the less he seems to understand that the psychiatrist does not "tell" you anything about yourself. The psychiatrist waits for the moment when you have sufficient strength and understanding to face some important fact of your unconscious life. Then he makes an interpretation of your behavior.

The psychiatrist's main role is to prevent the patient from continuing the self-delusions that serve to protect all of us from facing the truth about ourselves.

I have known persons who have been in analysis for years who, for one reason or another, may have to seek another analyst, but are loath to do so, because they feel their present doctor knows so much about them. I, too, faced this situation until I understood that inasmuch as I was handling my own cure, I could expect that any competent, trained therapist would have enough insight into my problems from one or two sessions to keep me from continuing my self-deception, hiding behind defenses that had made my life painful and frustrating (yet possibly served to prevent even greater pain).

To the question of what I got out of my experience with

psychoanalysis and psychotherapy, the answer is: "A great deal —but not enough."

The really unanswered questions are: What sort of person would I have been without it? Would I have survived? How much pain, fear, and loneliness did I prevent by going?

When I'm asked to answer these questions, I think of the story of the patient who broke his hand. As the doctor removed the cast, the patient asked, "Hey, Doc, will I be able to play piano?"

"Certainly," said the doctor.

"That's great!" said the patient. "I never could before."

No one questions physical medicine when bones don't heal, or illnesses persist, or function is not restored. Yet the same standard is not applied to psychoanalysis. There may never be answers. We don't know what the patient would have become without help, what potentials he might have developed above and beyond those that the treatment enabled him to fulfill.

I am sorry my treatment came before the days when group therapy came into its own. I have sat in group therapy meetings as an observer and seen how the members of the group can help one another. My own guess is that in some cases there is much more progress made at much less cost, depending on the skill of the therapist and the depth of the problem.

My perception of group therapy is that the emotions aroused are very much akin to those we all felt in the New York City blackout. We thought about and helped one another because we were all fellow sufferers.

My conclusions about analysis, from a completely personal point of view and a limited technical background, are (1) there is nothing wrong with psychoanalysis that more analysis for some analysts wouldn't cure, and (2) the technique used by the therapist is not as important as his understanding and warmth.

My experience has led me to believe that the best rule for the selection of a psychoanalyst or psychotherapist is your own intuition. If you feel, on first meeting him, "Here is a person who can help me," stay. Otherwise, go. Your intuition may be wrong but it's a better guide than anything I know, including the fact that the analyst has a high standing among his colleagues.

I believe that many psychologists, who lack a medical degree but are trained in psychoanalytic techniques, are possibly just as helpful as the psychiatrists who become psychoanalysts, and certainly less expensive. The psychologist is always conscious of the disapproval of the psychiatrist (because the psychologist doesn't have the snob appeal of a medical degree) and he doesn't assume the omniscient attitude that has become part of the stereotype we accept as the "psychoanalyst" with a medical degree.

But my analysis, I feel, did give me a most helpful technique for dealing with my own immaturity and self-centeredness. It taught me that I didn't have to allow my childhood to have such an undue influence on my adult life. Also, it gave me the understanding that anger, impatience, and rudeness displayed toward me by others is not my problem but that of the person indulging in such behavior.

To those who believe that drugs or other magic remedies can replace the long, expensive, painful road to self-knowledge, I can only ask, "Will the pill help us to love?"

A Twenty-Cent Bag of Candy
Floyd Patterson
By Lucy Freeman

Heavyweight champion of the world at twenty-one and the only boxer in his class to have regained the title after having lost it. Mr. Patterson is author with Milton Gross of an autobiography entitled Victory Over Myself.

"You can't say I've been on the couch. And I don't know exactly what you'd call the help I've received.

"But I know that I got on the right track because of the two years I spent at the Wiltwyck School for Boys. That's a place where they give help to boys in trouble.

"As a boy, I was in trouble. I stole and played hooky from school. But I never did again after I left Wiltwyck because of what happened there."

This is Floyd Patterson speaking. He was interviewed at his fight camp in Marlboro, New York, where he was in training for the bout against Cassius Clay, which was to take place on

November 22, 1965, in Las Vegas. Patterson, the only world's heavyweight champion who ever recaptured his crown was now preparing to regain it a second time.

On this September day, after he had gone a few rounds with a sparring partner, he sat in his room above the gymnasium and spoke of his life, before, during, and after Wiltwyck.

He was born near Waco, North Carolina. When he was about a year old, his parents moved to the Bedford-Stuyvesant section of Brooklyn where he grew up. They lived in one cold-water flat after another, always in need of larger space as more children arrived—eventually there were eleven in all. Floyd slept in the same bed wtih his two older brothers, Frank and Billy.

In his words: "I started stealing at the age of eight. I stole milk from the Sheffield Farms Milk Company for the family, and dresses for my mother, who never would buy herself a new dress. Once I broke into a dress store at two in the morning and stole a whole armful of dresses all the same size, my mother's size. I carried them carefully all the way home, taking special care when I had to jump over a wall.

"When my mother asked where I got the dresses and the milk, I told her I found them. But you can't keep on finding so many things. It's limited. Four or five bottles of milk a day and she got suspicious. She caught me after a while and forbade me to steal. But occasionally I'd steal milk anyway and put it with the rest of the food in the refrigerator, or put food I'd stolen in the cupboard, hoping she wouldn't notice. That way I was still able to bring in quite a bit of food."

He had feelings of guilt, he said, because his father worked so hard. "He not only worked six days a week," he said, "but even took another job on Sundays. Sometimes my mother worked, too. She took care of other people's children, or worked as a maid, or in a factory.

"I felt very, very sorry for my father. I'd see him go out to work at six in the morning and come home sometimes at one the next morning. Some days he'd take a drink when it was cold outside, after he got home. I was the one who would take off his shoes and clean his feet. I enjoyed it. Just like now, when I'm a father, I enjoy it when Jeannie, she's my six-year-old daughter, rubs my legs when I'm tired.

"Sometimes my father would drag himself home so tired he would just be able to hand his paycheck to my mother and sit down in a chair at the table, before he would fall asleep. I felt like a parasite. Here I was, not doing anything for the family. It was then I decided to steal. Sometimes I ran away from home, stayed a night or two, then came home with milk I had stolen. All the kids in the neighborhood stole. It seemed the thing to do if you were hungry."

At this point, Patterson said that the only way he could express how he felt about Wiltwyck was to explain how he felt about himself as a boy.

"I used to hate myself," he said. "My mother told me that when I was little, I would look at a photograph of my two older brothers, my younger sister and myself, hanging on the bedroom wall. I would point at myself and say, 'I don't like that boy.' One day, she said, she found three large X's that somebody—I don't remember doing it—had scratched over my face and body.

"I hated school. I felt I faced so many handicaps. I thought that I wasn't as good as the rest of the boys. I always felt like the dumbest one and acted like the dumbest one. I *was* dumber than the rest. Really. When I was nine years old, I didn't know I was nine years old. I didn't know the date of my birthday. I couldn't spell my name correctly. They didn't know my right last name at school for a long time because I spelled it wrong.

"I used to blame my mother for how I felt. I'm told that's a normal reaction for children. She did things to me that, at the time hurt very much. Although now I understand she couldn't have done anything else because we were so poor. For instance, my father, Thomas, was a longshoreman, a powerfully built man, almost six feet tall. Friday was assembly day at school and the boys had to wear a white shirt. My mother would take one of my father's shirts—it wasn't white, come to think of it, but off-white—and put it on me. My father had a 17½ neck and mine was about 14½. My mother would drape a tie around my neck, one of my father's big, fat ties, then pull it tight so you couldn't see how large the neck of the shirt was. But it still looked bulky. And when she tucked the shirt into my pants, it would then look funny around the waist. I felt ashamed and embarrassed as I walked off to school every Friday morning.

"The other boys would always break out laughing when I came into the room. At first I couldn't understand why. Then I realized they were laughing at the comical picture I made, and, I thought, the family from which I came. I began to draw back from everyone.

"I wanted my mother to let me quit school and get a job, but she wouldn't let me. She wanted me to have an education. But I couldn't see it her way. I kept on stealing and playing hooky."

Then one day he was caught, but good. "I was in a soda factory," he said, "lifting a case of soda. I was just leaving the factory, when a patrol car drove up. I started to run with the case of soda bottles. The patrol car had to pull up a long ramp and I thought I had time to get away.

"I ran, with a cop chasing me. He was catching up and I figured the heavy case was holding me back, so I dropped it, but first I grabbed two bottles to take home with me.

"But even those two bottles were heavy. So, as I ran, I dropped first one, then the other. I could usually get away by ducking into a subway, but this time the cop caught me. He got a good grip on me and hauled me back to the soda factory where the patrol car was parked.

'Why did you throw those bottles at me?' he demanded.

"He hit me with his fists. Then he picked up a crate and bashed me over the head with it. Luckily it was an empty crate, no soda bottles in it. I was groggy. But I kept insisting that I had not thrown the bottles at him, that I had dropped them as I ran because they were heavy.

"I was taken to court, before a judge who knew me. One thing on which I prided myself was always telling the truth. The judge knew this.

"I told him my story, how I had run away, first dropping the case, then the two bottles, and how the cop had hit me with the crate.

"At this point the cop stood up and, pointing at me, said, 'He's a liar. He *threw* the bottles at me. And I never hit him with a crate.'

"The judge said to the cop, 'You sit down. If Floyd says he dropped the bottles, he dropped the bottles. And if Floyd says you hit him with a crate, you hit him with a crate.'

"Then it was a pleasure going to jail, or what seemed to me at the age of ten, would be like jail. That judge could have sentenced me for life and I wouldn't have minded. He showed the world that he had faith in my word.

"In front of me and my mother, the judge suggested that I be sent to the Wiltwyck School for Boys in Esopus, New York. He told my mother that he thought the best thing for me was a place where my life would be more regulated. He asked her permission to send me to Wiltwyck.

" 'I know something's got to be done, Judge,' my mother said. She agreed I should go.

"Although at the time I resented being sent away from her, I am now very happy she gave her permission. Otherwise I might not have turned out the way I did.

"Before they took me away, she tried to talk to me and help me understand why I was going. She said it was for my benefit, that it was a very nice place where I would meet other boys and learn to get along with them, that I would be in a school where I would be taught to read and write. But all I knew at the time was that she and the judge were sending me away from home to a jail."

In September, 1945, Floyd Patterson was driven in a car with several other boys up the Hudson River, over a bridge at Poughkeepsie and westward into the hills to Wiltwyck, located on a 350-acre estate that once belonged to the Whitneys. He was frightened to death. He had never been away from home for more than a night or two when he had run away. He could not believe that Wiltwyck was not a prison surrounded by jailers.

"As we drove into the place," he recalled, "I saw four stone buildings, set against the green hills. I had expected to see fences around the property, and bars at all the windows, and guards standing at attention outside each building. But there were no fences, no bars, no guards. Instead there were barns, cows, and chickens, and Black Creek where the boys swam and fished. There was a classroom building, a craft shop, an art center, a big dining room and—most important for me, it turned out—a gymnasium.

"When I first arrived, I hated Wiltwyck, like any youngster would, sent away from home. I withdrew into a shell. But something happened after I had been there about two months.

"There was a teacher, Miss Vivian Costen, who tried to help me, and who seemed to like me very much. But I wouldn't let her break down the stone wall I had built around me, even though I knew I needed special help.

"There were eight boys to a class. She would sit and patiently explain things to us. But nothing got through to me. I wouldn't speak. I wouldn't ask questions.

"One day she asked all the eight boys a question. I forget what it was except it had to do with common sense, not book knowledge. The winner was to get a twenty-cent bag of candy.

"That appealed to me. I always loved candy. So I thought about the question and thought about it, and I believed I had the right answer. Then I thought, But I'm probably wrong and if I raise my hand and say the wrong thing, the class will laugh. So I said to myself, Forget it.

"None of the other boys gave the right answer, so Miss Costen told us the correct answer. It was the same as the one I had thought.

"I felt so bad that I jumped up and ran out into the hall. I had tears of anger and shame in my eyes for not speaking up.

"Miss Costen ran after me. After catching me in the hall, she put her hands on my shoulder and raised my head. 'Floyd,' she said softly, 'I knew you knew the answer to the question but you just didn't have the confidence to say it.'

" 'I was afraid I'd sound stupid and everybody would laugh,' I said.

" 'You're not stupid,' she said. 'And I want you to speak up after this, even if you think you are wrong. Everybody is wrong at times. You don't have to be one hundred percent right.'

"Then she said, 'I want you to have the candy.' She handed me the twenty-cent bag. I took it.

"From then on, I was happy at Wiltwyck. For the first time I felt there was someone I could talk to. If I didn't understand something in class, Miss Costen would go over and over it with me. She would never get angry because I didn't catch on right away. I started to speak up in class. I didn't care what the other boys thought. I just knew Miss Costen wanted me to speak out. Most of the time I had the right answer so I didn't feel stupid any more."

Each weekend Miss Costen would invite the boy with the best classroom performance to her house nearby. Patterson won that honor a couple of times and cherished those special days. In *Victory over Myself,* his autobiography, written with Milton Gross, published by Scholastic Book Services, he says:

"Miss Costen gave me confidence in myself. She made me feel I was important. She could tell that I was impressionable and a great sufferer. She knew that I was hurt by a raised voice. She wouldn't accept my protests that I couldn't learn to read or write. She was so kind and considerate and understanding that I wanted more than anything else in the world to please her. She bought me clothes and gave me little gifts. I had to return that to her in some way, and the only way I knew—or was able to—was to be what she wanted me to be."

She left Wiltwyck shortly after he did. She died about a year before he won the title. When he heard of her death, he felt a deep ache, he said, adding, "I think she would have enjoyed sitting in a ringside seat the night I knocked out Archie Moore and became champion at twenty-one."

It was at Wiltwyck that he first put on boxing gloves. The school offered many sports to keep the boys busy, including baseball, basketball, horseback riding, and swimming in summer. In addition, Walter Johnson, one of the counselors, staged boxing bouts three or four times a year.

One day Mr. Johnson asked Patterson if he would like to box in the tournaments. "I don't like boxing," the boy replied, "I don't want to go to the gym. I don't want to fight."

"Are you afraid?" said Mr. Johnson.

"I'm not afraid, I just don't want to," he said.

On one of her visits to Wiltwyck, Mrs. Patterson was informed by Mr. Johnson that her son did not join in sports much with the others. She said, "Maybe boxing will be good for Floyd. It might help him get the chip off his shoulder and be more like the other boys."

Patterson commented, "Maybe she was thinking of my two older brothers who were amateur boxers."

Mr. Johnson had to force Patterson to get into the ring for the first time, he recalled. He watched a couple of the boys box, then decided he would try it at Mr. Johnson's insistence. In one of the few letters he wrote his mother from Wiltwyck, he said, "Tell my brothers I'll join them in the ring some day." This was no idle prophecy.

He fought the first three bouts of his life at Wiltwyck. He won them all, although he didn't think he could beat the first boy—he remembers only that his name was Randolph. Randolph was bigger than he, and he had watched Randolph defeat several other boys. But he put on gloves and did not even feel afraid, he said, as he stepped into the ring and mildly lashed out at Randolph. When the fight was over, Randolph had a bloody nose and Patterson was unscathed.

When he fought, the boys would laugh because he had such a funny style. He jumped when he threw a punch. The sports writers later called this his "gazelle punch."

"All I knew was that the easiest way for me to get to my opponent was to jump up at him and throw the punch at the same time," he explained. "The only trouble was that sometimes I'd jump but miss with the punch and land on the floor. Then the boys would roar. But I didn't mind these laughs."

Many things about Wiltwyck surprised him, Patterson said, including the fact he was given a weekly allowance and the chance to earn extra money doing odd jobs. The boys ran their own canteen, elected their own student council and committees. If they had minor problems, they were encouraged to talk about them among themselves before seeking the help of a counselor.

"One thing really astounded me," he said. "I found it didn't make any difference that I was colored, the way it did in Brooklyn where white boys called me names. There were about thirty white boys, and forty to fifty Negro boys at Wiltwyck, and they all got along. I never heard one remark about the color of a boy's skin, or his religion."

In his book he tells how he made friends with both colored and white boys. His cot in the dormitory lay between a white boy named Galento and a colored boy named Saunders. At first, as always, he wouldn't say a word, just listen to them talk at night before they went to sleep, or watch them wage pillow fights. But then, after a month, he decided he wanted to be friends.

All the boys had work to do after school, like sweeping the floors or washing the walls, but when they finished they were free to roam wherever they wished over the spacious grounds. Patterson would see Galento go off by himself into the fields and forests, later to return with a snake or turtle or chipmunk. One day he asked if he could accompany Galento on his hike but Galento chased him away. Patterson asked again, another day. This time Galento said he could go along if he did not get in his way.

Galento taught him which snakes were poisonous, and how to catch harmless snakes, frogs, and other animals. He also taught Patterson to identify the different kinds of trees by their leaves. Patterson's love of nature and his desire to own a farm dates from those days of exploring the woods with Galento. He never saw Galento after they left Wiltwyck but Galento wrote him just before his first fight with Johannson, telling him he had become a big-game hunter (no surprise to Patterson in view of Galento's early forays into the wilderness of

central New York State) and was about to set off on a safari.
Patterson answered his letter right away suggesting they get
together, but concluded Galento must have left on the trip
before his letter reached him because he never heard from him
again.

Another thing that amazed Patterson about Wiltwyck was
the lack of punishment. No boy was ever whipped or locked up
for misbehaving. Dr. Ernst Papanek, noted for his compas-
sionate treatment of emotionally disturbed children, was then
executive director of Wiltwyck. He did not believe punishment helped a boy to understand why he rebelled. He believed
in proving to a boy that the school was trying to help him, not
hurt him more deeply.

Patterson says, "What I found at Wiltwyck was a sense of
belonging. I loved my mother and my father and my brothers
and my sisters. But I felt I also belonged to Wiltwyck. It helped
me feel the equal of the next guy. When the day came to go
home, I *did* want to go home, but I didn't want to leave Wiltwyck. I wanted both."

He also found that the nightmares he had all his life ended
at Wiltwyck. "At home, I would often have terrifying dreams,"
he recalled. "I would wake up screaming and in a sweat. My
mother would rush in, put cold towels on my forehead, and
hold me in her arms for a few minutes. Sometimes I would
walk in my sleep. Once my parents found me on the street,
walking along in a trance, wearing only the bottoms of my pa-
jamas. I have never walked in my sleep after leaving Wiltwyck."

Because he had done well at Wiltwyck, the school recommended that he get further individualized attention at one
of the "600" schools in New York City, then in the experi-

mental stage. There are fifteen today, but in 1947 when he attended P. S. 614, the Cyrus W. Field School, there were only two. One was at 113 East 87th Street, the other, where Floyd received his diploma, was at 113 East 4th Street.

At this school he found the same kind of understanding and sympathy that had helped him at Wiltwyck. He was chosen for an award as the best sport in the class one year. It was presented to him by Charles Schwefel, a member of the board of volunteer sponsors of the school, who owned and operated the Gramercy Park Hotel. Mr. Schwefel became a great influence in Patterson's life, encouraging him in his boxing career, which he started pursuing in earnest during his early teens, with the help of his older brothers. But the roots of his growing confidence in himself had been planted at Wiltwyck.

He next saw Wiltwyck when he was nineteen, just after Joe Louis presented him with a trophy awarded by the New York Boxing Writers as "Ring Rookie of the Year" for 1953. Up until this time, he had been fighting as a middleweight. Now he was ready for the light-heavyweight class, the 175-pounders.

Patterson was looking for a training camp where he could get ready for his fight with Joey Maxim, the former light-heavyweight champion of the world, but he couldn't seem to find a suitable place. He went searching for one in the hills across the Hudson, about seventy miles from New York City. Suddenly he realized he was near Wiltwyck. He stopped off to see some of his old friends.

Dr. Papanek was still there, as was Mr. Johnson. Patterson told them of his trouble in finding a training camp.

"Why don't you train here?" suggested Mr. Johnson, who served as resident director from 1954 to 1959.

Since Wiltwyck had a gym, boxing equipment, and country

byways for early morning roadwork, it seemed like a good idea, so Patterson trained at the place where he had first put on boxing gloves as a boy. (Maxim later beat him, his first defeat as a professional fighter, but he received solace from the fact that although the judges gave Maxim a unanimous decision, eleven out of twelve sportswriters at ringside were convinced that Patterson had won.)

Patterson has certainly repaid any debt he owes Wiltwyck. He is responsible for giving a very substantial sum of money for the establishment of an essential facility, called the Floyd Patterson House, at 208 East 18th Street, Manhattan. Opened in January, 1962, the House provides a place for twenty-five boys to live for six months at the end of their stay at Wiltwyck. Many of them need a period of time to adjust to city life before returning to their own homes or going into foster homes. At the Floyd Patterson House they may live, while attending public schools, and also have the benefit of a psychiatric social worker and remedial education staff. The House always keeps an extra bed or two available for any boy who, after leaving, feels the need to return for a night or so.

Shortly after Patterson regained his heavyweight title from Johannson he was guest of honor at a testimonial dinner, whose proceeds went to Wiltwyck. It was quite a night for him, he recalled, sitting on the dais with his mother, his mother-in-law (whom he says he loves almost as much as his mother), Mayor Wagner, James A. Farley, Jackie Robinson, Ed Sullivan, and other celebrities.

A cablegram from His Holiness, Pope John XXIII, conveyed papal blessings. Cus D'Amato, then Patterson's manager, presented him with a fourteen-karat gold crown set with diamonds, rubies, sapphires and pearls, and estimated at $35,-000. He was also given a portrait of himself painted by a student from one of the "600" schools. He felt, he said, as if he had come a long way from the frightened, speechless boy of ten who thought he was going to jail when he walked into Wiltwyck.

Wiltwyck taught him, among other things, to want to win. "I have never minded the personal sacrifice involved in training," he said. "Winning has been worth it. I fight for acceptance and recognition, so I can walk with anyone.

"I enjoy being a winner, and having people ask for my autograph. The day I stop being pleased, I'll know something is wrong.

"Some people think you have to hate to be a champion fighter. I have never hated an opponent except once. That was Ingemar, between the first and second fight. I hated him for a whole year, not because he beat me the first time, but because of his boasting on the Ed Sullivan program. He demonstrated on television how he knocked me out with his right-hand punch. I sat in my den and watched him on the screen and hated him as he laughed and joked. Because after he deprived me of everything I was, he seemed to be rubbing it in.

"And when he talked to the sportswriters at his training camp at Grossinger's, he seemed to speak of me with contempt, as though I were afraid of the second fight. He even called me a 'gymnasium fighter.'"

Patterson says he finds it hard to hate. "I feel that if a man hates, he can't have peace of mind," he declared. After he defeated Johannson in the return match, spinning him around in the fifth, then letting go with that final punch on the jaw that sent him to the canvas, Patterson recalled he was scared. Johannson was lying on his back.

"He wasn't trying to get up although the fight was over," he said. "I could see the blood slowly trickling from the corner of his mouth, and his left foot was shaking as though he was throwing a fit. I didn't know how hard my final blow had been—all I know is that I have never tried to throw a harder punch.

"Although I wasn't sure he could hear me, I ran over to Ingemar, lying there as his handlers, a doctor, and the referee bent over him, and said, 'You will get a third fight.'

"I had to say it. I wanted him to know he would have the opportunity to fight back, although he had not given me any such reassurance after my defeat. I had to spend lonely, desperate months wondering if I would ever get the chance at a return bout."

To make sure Johannson had heard him, Patterson repeated what he had said when Johannson finally got to his feet. "There was no more hate in me," he commented.

There was no hate either when Patterson fought Johannson the third time in Miami Beach. Patterson had trained long and hard for this fight and when he found himself hitting the canvas in the first round, he was disgusted, he said. He remembered the first fight when Johannson had knocked him down seven times.

"Somehow I had lost the style I had acquired for the second fight and I had to make a decision, one I had made many years before at Wiltwyck," he recalled. "I made up my mind, after being knocked down, to take the risk of getting hit with Ingemar's famous right hand. It was the only way I could get to him. It was like the risk I took at Wiltwyck one day when I climbed a very high wall. I stood on top, looking down at the ground, afraid to jump, yet wanting to. The more my fear grew, the more I wanted to jump. Finally I knew I had to take the chance of breaking an arm or leg. I closed my eyes and jumped. And I didn't get hurt.

"That night in Miami Beach, I decided to risk taking Ingemar's punches just so I could get at him. I managed to win. Yet I fought a very poor fight, in my opinion."

After the fight, Patterson walked over to Ingemar, threw his arms around him, and kissed him on the cheek, "much to the astonishment of the sportswriters," he says. "I guess it was an odd thing to do" he adds, "but I was telling him of my admiration. I thought he fought well. I admire much about Ingemar, aside from his ability as a fighter. For one thing, he is at ease in making public appearances, and I am not."

Before Patterson would sign for that third bout in Miami Beach, he insisted there be no segregation in the audience. A clause to this effect was inserted in the contract. It would have cost the promoters $10,000 in penalties if the contract had been broken. Patterson made them give him a check for that amount in advance, and the day after the fight, when he was satisfied that no segregation had taken place, he returned the check. He then contributed $10,000 to the National Association for the Advancement of Colored People, of which he is a life member.

Patterson has conquered much of his shyness. Occasionally a sportswriter will note that he will not look his opponent in the eye at a weigh-in.

"It's true, for some reason," he says. "But it's not true, as some of the writers said about my first fight with Liston, that I didn't look him in the eye because I was afraid. I just can't look *any* fighter in the eye before a fight. It doesn't seem right to be friendly and smile at a guy you intend to beat."

People have noticed that in the ring before a fight, Patterson kneels down and makes the sign of the cross. His family was Protestant and his mother, he says, "more or less made me go to church. I have had my own way of communicating with God, even though, as a child, things didn't always turn out the way I hoped they would. Sandra is Catholic and after we met, she tried to get me to become a Catholic. I resisted at first because I always feared the long black robes. But after I started to go to church with her, I saw the light, the peacefulness, and the simpleness of the church, and decided to become a Catholic.

"As I kneel in the ring I don't ask God for anything. Just to keep what I have. I pray that whoever the winner may be, both of us are able to walk out of the ring. Nobody has ever been badly injured in any fight I've been in."

What would he say to a youngster who felt as he did when he was nine?

"I think the message would have to be given to the adults around him. I would tell them to try to understand him, and how to treat him. I think they would be amazed how easily he would do small, simple things if he knew that the people he cared about believed in him. Most important is how the people he respects act around him—like the judge, Miss Costen, and my mother did, in my life.

"My mother deserves a tremendous amount of credit for

the way she brought us up. All eleven of us grew up to be healthy. My two older brothers have retired from fighting, but my younger brother, Raymond, now fighting in Sweden, has had fourteen professional fights. Maybe someday he'll be heavyweight champion.

"My mother lives comfortably in a home in Mount Vernon. Thanks to me? No. Thanks to her—that I was able to give it to her. She has become very active in the community which pleases me. I always wanted to see her going out and enjoying herself, which she now can do."

Patterson sums up, "I don't want to appear to feel sorry for myself, to have it seem that I suffered a lot when I was growing up. I have traveled all over the world and what I have seen of children in other countries especially in Egypt where nine and ten-year-olds fight in the streets for a scrap of food, makes me feel that I had everything as a child.

"But that doesn't take away from what Wiltwyck did for me. I had expected it to be a jail. Instead I found it full of people who liked and respected me. They were patient with me. They taught me right from wrong. They gave me a sense of the discipline that every fighter needs.

"At a time in my life when I could have gone one way or another, the right way or the wrong way, Wiltwyck headed me in the right direction."

A Statement
By William Inge

One of America's leading playwrights, Mr. Inge is best-known for Picnic, Bus Stop, Come Back Little Sheba *and* The Dark At The Top of The Stairs, *all of which were made into outstanding motion pictures. His most recent play is* Where's Daddy.

Psychoanalysis seems to me to be the great learning experience that the Twentieth Century can provide. Once one has worked through this experience, he cannot help but have a more basic understanding of human life and of all western culture. I do not think it is a necessary experience for all writers, and probably it is not a meaningful experience to anyone who does not seriously need it, but I believe that all writers who have undergone analysis have been grateful for its broadening influence upon their insight. Any analysand today can distinguish between those people prominent in our society and culture who have had experience "on the couch" from those who have not, and the former do appear to us more humane, more deeply aware of human needs, and more able to face the complexity of life today."

But Now I'm Proud of It
By Marjorie Lee

Marjorie Lee is the author of Games Analysts Play *and* Marathon 16 *with Dr. Martin Shepard and three novels,* The Lion House, The Eye of Summer, *and* On You It Looks Good, *and has written numerous short stories and poems for the leading national magazines. A former assistant editor of* Ladies Home Journal, *she resigned to get married. She is now writing another novel, two plays, and short stories. She also has written lyrics for songs that have been recorded by such stars as Dinah Shore, Peter Lind Hayes, Martha Wright, and Felicia Sanders.*

There was that time when I woke up, from God only knew what crippling dreams—in a beautiful house surrounded by lawn and trees, with a husband I'd married for love, and three healthy, great-looking children. And nothing moved. I was stopped dead, in the middle of my own clock. I had been underwound, or overwound—which of the two, or both at once, is no longer important.

Nor, does it seem, is the question: *Why did you go into analysis?* The answers are never true. To answer at all, you're forced to intellectualize; and that, in itself, is only a convenient method of distortion.

But say I've *got* to answer it. And today I do. Well, then—mustering up the deepest dregs of anything resembling basic truth—I went into analysis because I wanted to be perfect.

My childhood was no more, nor less, horrendous than anyone else's. Put all the childhoods of this book together, stir them up, add to them the countless case histories in the psychoanalytic files which haven't yet, and may never be, published. You end up with the same story: the ugly, beautiful, boring, thrilling, cowardly, courageous story of *people.*

Was my mother terrible, and was she wonderful? Did my father want me, and did he desert me? As an only child, was I both blessed and cursed? As a sibling, would my brother have been stronger than I, and my sister more beautiful?

Of course.

What have you got that I haven't got? A touch or a ton of murder? A thread or a rope of incest? Are you a thief and a liar? Somewhere within you is there an alcoholic, a drug-addict, a homosexual? Is it awful because you're a Jew or a Negro? Is it worse because you're not? Were you an orphan? Or did you only *wish* you were?

Is it coming clear now? Am I getting through to anyone? Usually, I don't. Usually I find myself having to repeat things a lot, having to say the same thing ten different ways. Not just to other people. To myself as well. It's amazing how hard it is to understand.

So, to reiterate: I went into analysis because I wanted to be perfect; because I actually believed I could be. "Just better" is the conscious wish. The wish that counts is deeper, more hidden. And long after I'd made that first terrifying trek to the couch, I learned that beside every rationale, beneath every sane-sounding reason for my need to be helped, lay the basic fantasy of perfection. *Here's the money,* I'd been saying in effect. *I'll pay and I'll stay until you give me what I want. It isn't much, and I'm sure you can do it: Make me happy. Make me wise. Make me beautiful.*

Dr. X was an imbecile. I tend to exaggerate. *Dr. X was not very bright.* Nor was he very "comfortable in his role." He was a blond, bland-looking Southerner who'd been psychiatrically trained within an inch of his life. He had gone through all the accepted schools, and earned all the accepted degrees. Having memorized every formula in the book, and mouthed every slogan on the Freudian billboard, he sat softly behind me, munching his luncheon sandwich.

I wanted desperately to love him. He wanted desperately for me to show my hate. After a couple of months of five hours a week, I did.

It took almost a year of successful, straightforward hostility to make him mad. One day I told him his neckties stank. There may have been no connection whatever, but on the following day, as I walked in—he kicked me out. (I learned later, with Dr. Y, that such terminations are usually precipitated by "unmanageable countertransferences.")

Dr. Y was my "real" analyst. I think of her as "real" because she stuck it out with me for nearly four years, kept a step ahead of me, parried my tricky sideswipes, refused my silences, plowed up the secrets of my unconscious mind, showed honest anger when I was an out-and-out brat, and honest warmth and sympathy when I was a lost little girl. It might be simpler to say that she was not only trained, but intuitive; that she not only worked, but cared. And still does, I would guess, even though I haven't seen her for over ten years. I know it's the dream of all analysands that their analysts will love them. Well, not every dream is bad.

If anything went amiss in my analysis with Dr. Y, it was finally, my inability to break loose from the transference. It had been a stormy one, fraught with overboard devotion, tangled in weeds of regressive dependency. In the year following my then-honorable discharge, and her removal to a city far in the West, I found the memories of that "perfect woman" weighing me down. It was a busy year for me: I had finished and sold my first novel, was working on my second; and I was pregnant with my fifth child. A rough time to be carting around an additional load of separation anxiety.

Dr. Z was older than Dr. Y; a strong, clear-cut, no-nonsense sort of woman whose own personal past of troubles had given her a sensible detachment. What a relief, and, oddly, what a brand new concept for me, when, one day during the course of my sit-up therapy, I had finished blurting out the "sordid" tale of a friend of mine who had been sexually lunged-at by her rabbi—only to have Dr. Z smile, cross her legs comfortably, take a deep drag on her dangling cigarette, and say: "Well, kid—that's life."

"What do you mean?" I said, openmouthed. "He's not just a rabbi, he's married!"

"So? Big deal, big deal. Gimme a ring and we'll set up another date in a couple of weeks."

"No! I've got to talk about this *now!*" (I was still, after all those years of deep analysis with Dr. Y, unconsciously saving small plums of reportage for the very ends of sessions in order to get ten or fifteen free minutes tacked on to my allotted fifty.) "That bastard is supposed to be a pillar of the community!" I insisted. "Don't you give a damn about Social Ethics?"

"Christ, Marge," she said, "you sure as hell get *grandiose* at times, don't you?"

Then she stood up, ushered me out of the office and walked me to the front door. As I left, she smiled again, easily, and said, "Look, kid—what I give a damn about is *life.*"

Of all the things that really counted in five years of on-and-off, face-to-face talk sessions with Dr. Z, the most important was her continued utterance of that single, common, yet overwhelming word: Life.

Shall I say now that my lousy start with X, my long and revealing search with Y, and my refreshing cleanup job with Z have left me cured? No. I'm alive—and, thank God, they haven't yet figured out a cure for that.

Dr. Y, in the deep analysis years, said once, out of a fear that I might, one day, emote myself square into a psychic crack-up, "You've got to be desensitized." Sometimes, I think, her caringness pushed her over to carefulness (a quite natural failing in mothers, whether they're your own, or temporarily filling in). In any case, I must reject that suggestion. Desensitization, the reaching of some permanent plateau of peace and passivity, is what I want least.

It *hurts* to respond to everything you see and touch and hear and smell. It hurts to read and think and watch what's going on. Who needed those pictures in *Life* magazine of the Congolese babies, starving in the road? Who wants to look at Ave-don's *Nothing Personal?* Four Negro kids got killed in an Ala-bama church. Walter Jenkins lost his job. The treatment for dope addiction is a jail cell. At Norristown State Hospital there's one psychiatrist for approximately three hundred and fifty patients.

What have *I* got to do with all that? Is it *my* problem? Yes, it is—because it's life.

Why should they expect me to sleep at night? How can any-one whose patron saint is Colette? At eighty-one, on her death-bed, her last word was: *Regarde.*

What's wrong with psychoanalysis? *That* is. It takes a good long look at life; but then it draws its limitations. It isn't true, what you read and hear about the absence of moralistic judg-ments, and the avoidance of fake societal pressures. I've never known an analyst who wasn't unconsciously pushing his or her own set of standards, swinging still, after all that drill and study, from the inner nooses of his own little background. Of all his worthy traits, objectivity allegedly heads the list. Yes, and he'll be the first to tell you so.

And then there are his revolutionary writings: new words, for the same old things. *Normal* is a corker: the twentieth cen-tury replacement for *Good. Perverse* is another: scratch it, you'll find *Evil.* No one's *Happy* anymore; they've all gone *Manic.* And whatever happened to true and decent and digni-fied *sorrow?* (Don't ask—it's too *Depressing.*)

On the other hand, I'm strong for my own humanness. Does it make sense, then, to expect more than that from anyone else? Am I free of making moralistic judgments? Am I, with my children, for example, above the selling of sermons on phoney rights and wrongs?

I try; but when I succeed, it's only intellectual. Deep down in the hidden corners of that implacable thing called Self, I *can* be shocked; I *can* be repelled. And with all the education I've had, all the flashy, gaudy sprints I've made away from the stifling hidebound attitudes and philosophies of my middle-class Russian Jewish background, there still lives within me the little girl who was supposed to be one thing above all others: *Nice*.

They did everything they could, didn't they? The best way they could. My mother was doing her best when she had my nurse teach me to handle an artichoke at the age of four so that whatever might befall me I would be equipped to "dine with the king of England." My father was doing his best when he accepted my mother's divorce decision and then went off, never to see me again. My grandmother was doing her best when she told me that "any girl who gives herself to a man before marriage can only go up to the top floor of the building and throw herself from the window." My grandfather was doing his best when he discharged his responsibilities as head of the household, and retreated for twelve years behind a wall of silent fury.

They all did the best they could, even though I want to scream and call it the worst. *You punished me when I was innocent! You said I was dirty when I was clean, chicken when I was brave enough to cry! You left me in my room at night and went out into your own world of marvelous grown-up grandeur. I was frightened, and you weren't there to hold me. You were big, I was little. You were beautiful, I was ugly. You didn't love me, you didn't love me, you didn't love me, LOVE ME! LOVE ME!*

They didn't love my analysts either. The analysts grew up

as I did, trying to get it made, one way or the other. But I think now that I may be more fortunate than they. I was a patient, as they were once, but one who didn't stay within the field. I could leave those couches and those offices, and travel beyond that one small facet of life which is The Problem—into a farther, larger place.

So, as I have tried to leave my parents, I try to leave my analysts. And, as it turns out, I'm not so damned nice after all. But the time has come for me to put up with me. Like the salesgirl who stands behind me as I try a new dress in the fitting room, it's time for me to look into that long, rather terrifying mirror, and say, "It's YOU, doll. . . ."

A year or so ago there was an article in the *International Journal of Psychiatry,* by Drs. Joseph Sandler and W. G. Joffe, of the Hampstead group. In it, they quote from Martmann, 1939: "A healthy person must have the capacity to suffer and be depressed."

Then there is my English friend, the novelist Shirley Verel. "Americans do appear rather to work on the assumption that everything regardless must somehow be 'fixed,' and that if you aren't fixing everything you're failing. I think what can be fixed, should be (i.e., teeth). I also think there will be in life as a whole, and in the individual lives of individual people, things which can't be fixed—and that to try can only make it worse. Therefore it seems to me that, in America, and elsewhere, the power of acceptance, of 'living with' where necessary, is an indispensable part of any personal philosophy."

I tried to hedge when she confronted me with that. I gave her the old argument about simply "wanting to be *better.*" But it *is* true: the Fix is on us, and until we can go through and beyond it, we're going to be stuck, each of us, with a personal unreality. Women, especially, and especially—here. One of these days, or aeons, the subject of the American Woman may well beat out Integration and Vietnam as national muck-up no. 1.

Our framed degrees, the work accomplished in science labs, courtrooms, schools, and offices, are external and manifest proof of our progress. (These thoughts are taken from an article, "The Hidden Dissuaders," which I wrote for the Sarah Lawrence College alumnae magazine of May, 1965.) But *internally* it's still an accepted all-American "fact" (however lightly and jestingly expressed) that women are people who bear children, wear crazy hats, cause traffic jams, and hold everyone up while they yammer on the golf course.

While the Successful Woman image is touted for all its worth on TV panel shows, radio, and lecture platforms, its inner frailty can be calibrated by its nervous response to one small narrowing of eyes across a room, one quick curl of the mouth, one sigh of exasperation; one sentence: "Well, you know *women*. . . ." In toto, American women, at the bottom of their hearts and psyches, are just about as emancipated as they were before they won the vote.

Who's responsible? American men? That's the easiest answer, of course. But it isn't by a long shot, the valid one. Men are neither the cause of female sabotage, nor the kind, understanding alleviators of it. It's the female herself who, in a neurotic attempt to retain her alleged psychological status as the Real Woman, stands around waiting to be sabotaged: by her husband, by her children, and by any of her female neighbors who happen to be pounding dough instead of a typewriter.

While pointing our ship forward, we hang on behind it, playing, all by ourselves, and for ourselves, the role of hidden dissuaders.

How did it happen? We seemed to be doing so well. We had passed the fitful, fightful times of the bloomers and the placards and the shouting in the streets for rights and equality. We had won. The polls opened, the universities opened, the world opened. The feminist faded. Having done her job, her exit from the scene was logical.

Why, now, the entrance of the neofeminists: the Marya Manneses and the Betty Friedans? Well, crusaders arise to speak only when called upon by times and circumstances. Even lunatic fringes are attached by some very solid stitching to the seemingly sane whole. Somewhere along the line, the snag occurred. We went from serf to feminist to flapper to careerist. The last of those stages is the one I remember best. Hollywood, that bull in our cultural china shop, has a way of touching the pulse of things, however tastelessly. In those days of the thirties it was hard to find a movie in which Fred MacMurray, applying for a job, didn't discover that the head of the company was Rosalind Russell.

And then someone got psychoanalyzed.

Gertrude Lawrence, to be exact.

Gertrude Lawrence was very busy running this big fashion magazine: efficient, smart, chic. But one day she found herself smack in the middle of a terrible depression. Headaches, as I recall; insomnia; chain-smoking. It all became too much to cope with, so she went to see somebody named "Dr. Brooks." There was this couch in his office. And wham!—before you could even adjust your seat and open your program, you realized that with all this success she had had, with all the money she was making, she was, deep, deep down where it matters, nothing but a "lady in the dark." Never in all those years of the big time had she ever known what it was to be a real woman.

I saw the show while I was in college. It made me cry. But I didn't quite know what I was crying about until years later, when I too was psychoanalyzed, only to find that Gertrude Lawrence and I had the same problem.

If I keep sounding like a jibing debunker of Freud, it's only because, often, I am one. But not by any means a total dissenter. There's no question that Freud changed the course of the Western world by evolving a method by which to reach, uncover, and explore the unconscious mind. I've been reminded frequently that "Dostoevski knew a lot more about the unconscious than Freud ever did." Be that as it may, Dostoevski didn't leave the know-how behind; Freud did.

Acceptance of his genius might well rest on that contribution alone. Unfortunately, he made a few others. And one of them was a complex of formulations leading up to the concept of the Real Woman.

Psychoanalysis is mostly a matter of Feel Now, Think Later. Well, now it's later, so I'm thinking: the Real Woman of Freud's time was the product of the Victorian era.

Our error lies in our failure to differentiate between his science and his personal attitudes. The basic points of the science are vital; the attitudes, however, thoughtlessly backed up and perpetrated by many analysts, are causing a good deal of trouble.

There's no need for the use or even the conscious understanding of Freudian terms like *passive-receptive* versus *active-aggressive,* or feminine *maso*-something as opposed to masculine *sado*-something else. With or without the words, we've all gotten the pitch somehow. We know what we're "supposed" to be, and, even more acutely, what we're "not supposed" to be. A dozen times a day we turn inner handsprings and stand on our emotional heads in order to fill the bill. To paraphrase Mary Bunting, our greatest waste of women is energy—used up in self-defense, attempts to justify, and the urgent placation of anyone at all who seems, even slightly, to "disapprove."

We're getting the degrees all right, and, slowly, the available jobs are being shared. But, tied by invisible strings to an outdated mold, we wonder, and, knowingly or not, we're afraid. Disapproval, after all, may lead to loss, loss to sadness or anger, anger inevitably to guilt, guilt to confusion, and confusion to the start of the same cycle all over again. For what? The Good Housekeeping Seal of Approval? The seal of approval *is* essential; the mistake is in expecting it to come from *Good Housekeeping.* To have meaning, to last, it's got to come from ourselves.

It's difficult, when you're writing this sort of piece, to skip, completely, the marital area. After all, I did keep dragging it to the couch like a half-dead horse, hell-bent on vocalizing its disasters. The end-product of all that verbiage was a single basic insight: focusing on the faults and failures of the other person leads nowhere. Your husband will never be your father, or your brother, or God. Nor will he ever be St. Francis, feeding the little birds, of which you are one.

What he's likely to be is a pain in the ass. But very much less so if you can learn to accept him as a human being. Don't want always, and try always, to change him. You got him from the "as is" department. So keep him and shut up; or dump him. But don't expect him to change.

There was a time when I thought my husband was seeing another woman. I ran to Dr. Z and shot off a rocket of surprise and dismay and hurt feelings. She sat there, as usual, with the dangling cigarette, and said, "Jesus, but you're naive. What's the big deal about faithful or not faithful?"

So, parroting from my analysis with Dr. Y, I said, "But infidelity is a manifestation of unresolved Oedipal conflict."

"Yeah, sure," she said. "And I think it would be lovely, perfectly *ideal*, if all the needs two people had could be taken care of under one roof. But I don't know one roof in this whole damn world that's covering it all, do you?"

And, no—I didn't.

I saw her for five hours, in the space of three days, working that one out. And then I went home and looked at my husband and thought, *I won't bother you with this crap anymore. Not ever again.* Because the gift of love has in it, must have in it, the gift of freedom. Wanting to tie someone up, chain someone, write out the day's or night's *orders* for someone, isn't love at all; it's hate.

Whatever my husband has, whatever he learns, whatever joy there is for him, it'll come home to me in some way—if I *let* it. What do women want from men? Do we want them to anoint us, for God's sake? Where did we ever get the idea that anyone *owes* us fidelity, or that *in*fidelity proves an absence of love?

Did my analysis "work"?

Twenty-five percent of it did. Seventy-five percent of it

didn't. But then, as the businessman said—you can't go broke making a profit.

I still quake at the thought of a literary lunch with my agent, or an editor. I go through the tortures of hell before speaking publicly. I worry like crazy about my children. I use up months of energy at a time, fighting my writer's block instead of writing. I don't eat regular meals. Getting up in the morning feels like the start of a death march. I wear dark glasses when I can get away with it. I go haywire over the most lost and obscure of causes. I'm one-half to one hour late to almost everything. I abhor large parties of people I don't know intimately. I can live for six months without making the beds if there's no one else to make them for me; yet my compulsion for neatness when I'm writing is little short of insane. I take two-hour baths, often twice a day, leaving my family to throw screaming fits, and my enraged friends to make repeated phone calls in order to reach me. I find it hard to compete against women, particularly when I know I can win. Trembling, I play parlor word-games for money, and blood. I keep getting into debt with art galleries. I sweat with anxiety in a dentist's chair, even when it *doesn't* hurt. My relationships are apt to be complicated, and in the end a good many of them take more out of me than they return. I get seasick. The list of residual problems is endless. But, just possibly, the most basic one of all is the fact that while most of my life holds to an external framework of everything that is normal and right and acceptable, inside I have flatly refused to conform.

I've come to see existence as a long corridor of doors. I want to open them. Some of them have been, and will be, great; there's the beauty one, the love one, the wisdom one.

But there are others, behind which, I know, lie the grim surprises. The last of those doors is called Belief. My fantasy is that it leads off into a small alcove in which stands an old Salem stake, rigged and prepared with a waiting supply of twigs and brushwood.

Sometimes I can smell my own smoke.

I'm hardly the answer to an analyst's prayer.

It's another day now; and I'm home. It's afternoon. I've just reread all this, and I'm struck with the changes of mood—even, in spots, of viewpoint. In terms of the clear, cohesive quality essential to any piece—reportage or fiction—it fails. I've written the things which have come to mind *as* they came to mind . . . with the exception of one section in the middle that was put in later. The people and the activities that have interrupted and divided me, and the several sessions of typing, have left their mark, ghostlike, between the lines.

This can't be called free association, because, to a large extent, I've been conscious of filling an assignment. Still, I've kept the editing to a bare minimum, and there's been more freedom to let it just happen, any way it wanted to, than I'd ordinarily allow myself in writing for publication.

Maybe, for this book, it's better that way. Maybe these inconsistencies and lapses of form are echoes of the thing I've wanted most to say: that the deliberate and circumscribed search one makes for one's self in psychoanalysis must end in openness and the ability to embrace the vast, sprawling, often untidy whole. Because, as Dr. Z, with her freed-up, offhand, cigarette-dangling smile informed me—"Well, kid . . . that's life."

Why Me?
By Arthur E. Meyerhoff

Mr. Meyerhoff is a nationally known leader in the advertising profession, head of the Meyerhoff Advertising Agency in Chicago. He is author of the recent book, The Strategy of Persuasion, *and has lectured widely throughout the country.*

I entered the advertising business in 1929 at the time when the theory of the unconscious was first being employed by the advertising profession. By understanding the unconscious motivations that entered into people's selection of certain products, the advertising copywriter could more easily key his appeals to the needs of the purchaser. Naturally, I read every book I could lay my hands on and, in a sense, considered myself an amateur psychoanalyst.

The organization I headed was among the first in the business to make use of motivational research. When we encountered more complex problems, our agency consulted with the late Dr. Franz Alexander, founder and director of the Institute for Psychoanalysis in Chicago, who checked our findings.

To my sorrow, I found it was a great deal simpler to come to conclusions on products than to understand myself in my relationships with others. As a result of my association with psychoanalysts and the great amount of analytic literature I had read, I felt I had a perfect understanding and control of myself.

I often had the urge to go through psychoanalysis, not to solve any personal problem I had, but to become more proficient in understanding and handling others. Never, at any time, did I consider it from the viewpoint of my own neurotic needs.

One day, after a conflict with a business associate who, according to my diagnosis, was emotionally disturbed, I sought the help of an eminent psychoanalyst, Dr. Thomas French, of the Chicago Institute for Psychoanalysis. I wanted his advice on how to handle this man without jeopardizing his value to the company. After a fifty-minute consultation, Dr. French set me back on my heels by saying calmly, "I think, Mr. Meyerhoff, you could benefit from a diagnostic analysis."

Quite naturally, my reaction was, "Why me? I came to see you about my associate."

It took several days to overcome the shock. Then I found myself calling Dr. French and asking him to recommend a psychoanalyst. He suggested that I see Dr. George Mohr, also of the Chicago Institute, for my "diagnostic analysis."

I saw Dr. Mohr—five times a week for two years. I would go to his office early each morning before my business day began.

In retrospect, while I had believed I was able to function normally in most of my relationships prior to my analysis, I realize now I was incapable of relating intelligently when faced

with the temper tantrums of my business associate. I was able
to do so only after I understood myself better. Then I realized
that to become a party to a heated exchange, one is also a par-
ticipant. As long as he participates, reacting to the provoca-
tions with which he is presented, he is in trouble. It is comparatively easy to remove oneself from an aggravating situation
if possessed of the emotional strength to do so. As they say, it
takes two to fight successfully. If one withdraws in understanding, there is no fight.

The results of my analysis were not earthshaking. The
knowledge I gained did not seem to benefit me in any important way. But I believe analysis prepared me to handle the
problems I faced during the next twenty years and has probably made the difference in my being here to enjoy an active
life. Not until later did I realize how many anxieties I had
within myself—anxieties that had affected almost every trans-
action or exchange I conducted with other people.

I understood myself much more as I looked back at my early
life. For instance, I recalled that when I was four years old, a
neighbor stayed at our home because she had been abandoned
by her husband. She brought with her a young son, a pale and
sickly boy, whom I remembered as extremely sad. The woman
was bereft, telling us all of her plight rather tearfully. Consciously, I had never felt very involved in their tragedy. But in
telling this story during analysis, I reacted with strong feelings.

I had obviously deeply identified with the pale, sickly, sad,
abandoned boy. The effects of the incident had been so profound and lasting that, throughout my entire life whenever
there was a possibility of a frustration, regardless of the outcome, I became the abandoned little boy.

The process of psychoanalysis was to reeducate me, at least insofar as my unconscious was concerned; to help me realize I was an adult, able to meet frustrations and losses without overreacting, as I had done all my life. This overreacting had never been apparent to those on the outside, but it had created many sleepless nights and days of suffering.

This identification with the deserted little boy, while probably the most important single discovery made during my analysis, was followed by other smaller recollections which took hours and hours to bring up from my unconscious. Because I had heard stories about people who became so overwrought during their analysis that they behaved erratically, I wondered from time to time why I experienced only relief during my sessions. It was explained that every analysis does not follow the same course.

As a result of my own experience, I became interested in helping others if they asked for it. When they came to me for guidance, that guidance now was, "Go see a professional."

The manager of a baseball club, who knew I was interested in psychoanalysis, asked my advice about a talented baseball player. This young man had all the physical attributes to be a successful pitcher in the big leagues but temperamentally seemed unfitted to do so. He had a history of walking off the ball field and going home if the umpire made a call with which he disagreed.

The club manager asked my recommendation. I suggested that the ball club make psychoanalytic help available to the player during the off-season. He was willing to see a psychoanalyst, and after receiving help for two years, the young man became a major league baseball pitcher and, subsequently, left baseball to become a successful author, as well as a radio and television personality. (Since Jim Brosnan gave me credit for suggesting he go to a psychoanalyst, in an article that appeared in *The Saturday Evening Post* in 1961, and does it again, elsewhere in this book, it is no secret that he is the man to whom I refer.)

Not everybody can use the help of psychoanalysis. As the result of my success in guiding Jim, another baseball player who was not the star he should have been on the field, was sent to me and I again recommended psychoanalytic help. After a diagnostic analysis, the analyst who interviewed him reported that he was so normal that absolutely nothing bothered him. Perhaps because of his extreme normalcy, he never did become a successful player.

During my analysis, although I knew very little of Dr. Mohr's personal life, I felt that I knew *him.* I was aware of an inner presence, so to speak—of his deep interest in helping me, and his profound dedication to his profession. I always felt very warm and friendly toward him. Many friends have talked to me about the pain they endured during their analysis. I can truthfully say that I found analysis very supportive and decidedly not painful. At the beginning of my work with Dr. Mohr I had anxiety dreams, but as time went on my dreams became serene, often happy.

Dr. Mohr never used psychological jargon during our hours together. I was surprised and pleased that he spoke to me in lay terms. I understand this is accepted practice among analysts today, but in the late thirties and early forties it seemed that everyone who was in analysis, or had been in analysis, peppered his speech with the technical terminology he learned from his psychoanalyst.

An experience at the end of my analysis is worth recounting.

While psychoanalysts rarely give personal advice, on this occasion Dr. Mohr explained that he was stepping out of the role of a psychoanalyst to give me what he thought was practical guidance.

I had to make one of the most important decisions of my life in 1945—whether to marry for a second time. Naturally, the subject came up during an analytical hour. In discussing this problem, Dr. Mohr said, "I'm going to step out of the role of psychoanalyst and advise you directly. I feel that you should not take such a major step at this point in your analysis."

Despite his advice, I decided to remarry. I felt certain it was the right thing for me to do.

Once I made the decision, Dr. Mohr said, "We can now talk about terminating. You have been able to consider the move and make your own decision in spite of my suggestion that you wait. I am pleased at your strength. You no longer need me."

I can honestly say that my second marriage might not have been a success without the insights I gleaned from analysis. My work with Dr. Mohr (who has since died) enabled me to be objective—at least a bit more objective than I could have been otherwise—about my relationship with my second wife and eventually with our daughter.

Often I have been asked what I felt were the results of my analysis. Obviously, it has not transformed me. But I feel that analysis has given me another dimension, a bit of an edge, so that now I'm able to look at a problem on more than one level. As I can step back and view the situation objectively. I can bring my full faculties to bear on a solution. This is a very rewarding feeling—a feeling of being master of a situation, not slave to it.

The Sensitive Genius
Josh Logan
By Lincoln Barnett

One of Broadway's top directors, Mr. Logan has staged such hits as Mister Roberts, South Pacific—*both of which he co-authored*—Annie Get Your Gun, Fanny *and* Picnic. *He has also directed such screen favorites as* Bus Stop *and* Sayonara.

Josh Logan and I knew each other at college, where we had met through our common interest in the Triangle Club. But for more than fifteen years thereafter we never laid eyes on each other, although we both worked in New York, most of the time only a few blocks apart—he in the precarious caverns of the theater district and I on its journalistic periphery. I saw several of the shows he directed and was aware of the general upward movement of his career, but for some reason or other our trails never met. One evening shortly before the war I ran into a mutual friend who asked me if I had heard about Josh. He looked very serious, and I said, "No, what's happened to him?"

197

"He's cracked up," he said.

"What?"

"He's off his rocker. He's in an institution."

"What do you mean? Did he have a nervous breakdown?"

"Worse than that, I guess." He went on to say that no one knew any details, but it appeared the phrase "nervous breakdown" was only a euphemism for the sort of disturbance from which Josh was suffering. He didn't know the cause—it did not seem to be alcohol—but the effects were severe enough to leave some question as to whether his promise had not been wrecked, permanently. This seemed incredible to me, for like any half-educated layman I had a preconception of the type of person who might be susceptible to that kind of breakdown: the so-called "neurotic type," anemic, ascetic, introverted, antisocial, solitary. Josh had none of these qualities. He was indeed their very antithesis—he was burly, outgoing, uninhibited, warm-hearted, gay-spirited, gregarious, a big, confident, noisy guy with a big laugh and a knack of getting laughs from others. The very idea of his succumbing to a mental disorder seemed so improbable that I inclined to discount the story as a piece of Broadway hyperbole, and by the next morning I'm afraid I had almost forgotten it. Time moves quickly in journalistic work, and acquaintances are numerous and fluid, so that months passed before I heard any word of Josh again. My work did not touch the theater at the time; I was a news editor and the news was terrible. Then one day I spotted an item in the drama pages announcing that Joshua Logan had been engaged to direct the new Rogers and Hart musical, *By Jupiter.* I remembered the gossip about his breakdown and guessed it must have been fictitious, or colossally exaggerated, after all. Soon after that I heard he had gone into the Army.

When the war ended, a combination of circumstances brought me in touch with Josh again. First, quite by chance, I came to know his mother and sister, whom I had never happened to meet when he was at college. Then I began seeing Josh and his wife from time to time in the course of my work, which had begun to veer toward the theater. He had changed somewhat—but, then, so had I. And the warmth and the laugh were still there. The winter of 1947-48 was an important one for Josh, not only because an unbroken series of postwar successes had established him as the currently top-ranking director on Broadway, but because he at last made his debut as a playwright. It was quite a debut, for the play was *Mr. Roberts*. As one consequence of its huge success, the editors of *Life* scheduled a piece about Josh and asked me to do it.

The prospect of spending the long reportorial hours with someone I knew and liked and with whom I had common interests, mutual memories, and no sense of professional formality was something new in my experience and vastly more attractive than the stew of diffidence, anxiety, and stage fright with which I ordinarily approached each new assignment. But the outcome was utterly different from anything I had imagined. I had presupposed that my only problem would be to examine Logan's distinction as a director—and in doing so to answer the question, obscure to even regular theatergoers, of precisely what a director contributes to a play. Essentially the story would be semitechnical in mood, concerned chiefly with the aesthetics of dramatic art.

That the story evolved so differently from all my preconceptions was the consequence of a personal decision by Josh. I had almost forgotten, or at least relegated to the status of a minor episode, his breakdown before the war. Yet the gossip had not been exaggerated; his illness had been a terrifying one, and every phase and emotion remained knife-sharp in his memory. For several reasons Josh determined to disclose this entire experience from beginning to end and let me use whatever I saw fit. One motive was his desire to set forth in accurate detail what had been circulated in whispered and distorted conjecture along Broadway for seven years. But his major purpose was selfless; at the onslaught of his illness he had stubbornly resisted certain measures which he felt now had been instrumental in saving his sanity and perhaps his life; he wished to affirm the value and necessity of those measures, and to emphasize by his own example the possibility of emerging from the darkest defiles of the mind into the full sunlight of normal life, health, and professional achievement. It is a characteristic of manic depressives—which Josh was—to fight virtually to the point of death against hospitalization; the grim irony of their condition is that their commitment must be voluntary to be effective. In recent years the psychiatrist to whom Josh gives grateful credit for his recovery, Dr. Merrill Moore of Boston, has several times called on him to testify to patients and help them understand in the light of his experience that only by committing themselves could they hope to get well. Josh had responded whenever Dr. Moore had made this request. His conviction now was that publication of his story could benefit many more in the same way.

Unlike many men of sensibility, Logan can look back to a childhood which was both tranquil and gay. He grew up in Louisiana swaddled in all the clichés of the South—a rambling house hung with wisteria and circled by fields of cotton and sugar cane, a Negro mammy, possum hunts, barbecues, holly trees at Christmas, etc., etc. Since his father died when Logan was a small boy and his sister Mary Lee but six weeks old, his interests were shaped chiefly by his mother, who was (and is) a deeply sensitive votary of beauty in nature and in art. Instead of Mother Goose she taught him Shakespearean songs, so at the age of four he could trill, "Hark, hark! the lark at heaven's gate sings, and Phoebus 'gins arise." She impressed on him the virtues of consideration and compassion for others; when he fell and bumped his head she would admonish him, "But think how Mr. Floor feels," and he would sob, "Forgive me, Mr. Floor." One day when he and his sister were old enough for movies she took them to a Biblical picture called *Judith of Bethulia*. As the film neared its climax she saw to her dismay that the Assyrian, Holofernes, was going to be beheaded right before the eyes of Josh and Mary Lee. Seizing them in either hand she thrust their faces down into her lap an instant before the ax fell. "Think of fields of yellow daisies. Think of fields of yellow daisies," she whispered hypnotically. The phrase has been a family motto ever since. Years later, when their step-father died, Logan and Mary Lee sent their mother a telegram reading simply, "Think of fields of yellow daisies."

Logan showed symptoms of the impresario before he had started school. He composed allegories and staged them in the back yard, with Mary Lee in supporting roles. One day he told his mother he would require a dog suit for school the next morning. "Now, how am I going to get you a dog suit?" she protested, "Why, just go downtown and buy some dog cloth," he said. She pieced together a tolerable dog suit out of some brown flannelette and only learned afterward there had been no school play as she had believed; Josh had simply decided to dramatize his reading lesson, which was about a dog. "It was sensational," he recalls.

When his mother remarried, a powerful new influence entered Logan's life. His stepfather was Colonel Howard F. Noble, a staff officer of Culver Military Academy. By then Josh was eleven years old, a big boy but rather flaccid. He knew that "Dogs fight, gentlemen don't"; he signed his name J. Lockwood Logan III and was an honor student at Mansfield Female College, a regrettably named institution consisting of a teachers' college with a grade school attached. Although Colonel Noble was a man of cultivated tastes, interested in the theater, talented as a painter, and convinced, as he once wrote, that "all the beauty that can be crowded into a boy's life is needed, for God knows life itself is hard enough," one of the first things Colonel Noble did on getting his new family settled at Culver was to arrange boxing lessons for Josh. In a short time Logan had a new ambition: to be tough. He cultivated a Hoosier accent in place of his Louisiana drawl. He worked hard at his boxing, did roadwork before breakfast, and took a correspondence course with Muscle Builder Charles Atlas. Ultimately he became light heavyweight champion of the academy, though he was nervously sick before every bout. He also played tackle on the football team, wrote a column for the campus newspaper, won a medal for declamation, and dominated theatricals. Although in his first role, a butler, he found his offstage waits so intolerable that he wandered on during a climactic scene just to be there, he was soon playing leads, which enabled him to be onstage most of the time. He was awarded a special prize on his graduation for leadership in the cultural activities of Culver Military Academy.

At Princeton, which he had elected to attend because of the theatrical lure of the Triangle Club, Logan remodeled his personality a second time. Discovering that his Indiana twang and seminars with Charles Atlas did not impress his urbane classmates from eastern schools, he soon mastered East Coast diction and the technique of being "smooth." At the end of his freshman year he teamed up with a junior named Erik Barnouw (now a radio author) to write the next year's Triangle show. Into it Logan introduced a character so adapted to his own talents that when casting started everyone agreed he was a natural for the part. As a result he was the star as well as co-author of the show in his sophomore year; and in his senior year he became president of the Triangle Club, thus attaining what had always seemed to him the *ultima Thule* of human destiny. In their senior poll the class of '31 voted Logan "wittiest," "thinks he's wittiest," "most original," and "thinks he's most original."

The most important influence Logan encountered during his college years was not the Triangle Club bu the University Players, an intercollegiate group founded by Charles Leatherbee of the Harvard Dramatic Club and Bretaigne Windust, Princeton '29, now well known on Broadway as director of *Life with Father, Arsenic and Old Lace,* and other hits. They had a theory that college actors were handicapped in the theater by a time factor: they were four years too late in getting started. The summer theater they set up at West Falmouth, Massachusetts, initially for college players only, held together less than five seasons, but its impact on the theater and Hollywood is still evident. It inaugurated the careers of Henry Fonda (Minnesota), James Stewart (Princeton), Margaret Sullavan (Sullins), Mildred Natwick (Bennett), Myron McCormick (Princeton), Kent Smith (Harvard), and Norris Houghton (Princeton), among many others. Indirectly it insinuated intelligence and taste into a business which often lacked those elements. The University Players were not highbrows; they wanted commercial success, but they also had ideals. They built their own theater and scenery; their credo was *Get in there and act*. "We all knew we had talent," Fonda recalled in later years, "and so we took it for granted—we never praised anybody, and we were merciless in our criticism. Everyone's worst fear was the disapproval of the company. If someone was bad, we tore him to pieces. Only the strong survived."

From their first meeting at the University Players, Fonda and Logan impressed each other as hilarious clowns and they operated together for a while as a successful comedy team. Fonda soon drifted into serious roles, however, and Logan somewhat later into directing. In this relationship they often found themselves at odds, and on one occasion Actor Fonda led a group of the Players in revolt against Director Logan. Though they remained good friends—Logan was best man at Fonda's marriage to Frances Brokaw—they did not work together again in the theater till their reunion in *Mr. Roberts*.

Apart from the University Players the most valuable opportunity that came Logan's way at this time was a scholarship entitling him to a season of study with the Moscow Art Theater. Although it meant renouncing his final term at Princeton and hence his degree, Logan left for Russia in the spring of 1931, accompanied by Charles Leatherbee, and spent the summer under the tutelage of Constantin Stanislavsky, the Moscow Theater's great founder. Stanislavsky was the subverter of classical tradition in the theater, the archenemy of artificial forms, meaningless conventions, and everything studied, posed, or unfelt. Working always for the true, believable emotional effect—the "incandescent experience"—he dedicated every dramatic technique to the attainment of veracity. His theories on opera, which he transformed from a costumed concert into a sung drama, are embodied in Logan's handling of musicals, which are all distinguished by rich character development, full exploitation of emotional values, and effortless transitions between musical numbers and scenes.

Logan and Leatherbee returned from Russia ablaze with exalted ideals for the American stage. Hoping to affirm them through the University Players on a year-round basis, they took over a theater in Baltimore. But by then the United States was deep in depression and, after a winter of fluctuating hopes, deficits, and submarginal existence, the Players dissolved and straggled into New York one by one to look for jobs. "Those were the days of the trek," Logan later recalled, referring to the daily fruitless rounds of agencies and casting offices. The irony of their situation was that no agent would handle an actor he had never seen perform, and no agent had ever seen or heard of Henry Fonda, James Stewart, Joshua Logan, or the others. They met for lunch each day at a drugstore in Times Square and drank beer one night a week in a bar off Eighth Avenue. Logan's ambitions had not entirely crystallized at this time. While he loved to act, he felt at ease only in grotesque character parts. But when he tried to enact any role that approximated himself—an American in his middle twenties—he began worrying about his looks, which have always displeased him. His hopes of becoming a director, however, had been undermined by Fonda, who had repeatedly urged him to relinquish that idea for his own good.

In the midst of this bleak period his stepfather died and his mother came to New York to live with him. (His sister Mary Lee had meanwhile married Charles Leatherbee.) One day just before his mother's arrival he went into a telephone booth with five nickels and vowed he would come out with a job or quit the theater. He invested his first nickel on Howard Lindsay, who had just written a comedy about Princeton called *She Loves Me Not*. Lindsay told him apologetically he had nothing better to offer than a position as understudy and sixth assistant stage manager at $25 a week—and advised him not to accept. Logan feels his decision to take the job was the crucial decision of his career. *She Loves Me Not* ran for months, and by the time it closed Logan had risen to stage manager, which enabled him to obtain subsequent jobs at that level.

About the time he became bored with backstage management he received simultaneous offers to direct two separate shows and he snatched both. In the mornings he worked on a play called *Hell Freezes Over;* evenings he went to Princeton to direct the Triangle show, *Stags at Bay*. This double duty and the traveling it involved took a toll of his health and confidence. At one morning rehearsal his friend Myron McCormick who was playing in *Hell Freezes Over,* started an argument of the kind the University Players used to have regularly. "Please don't argue with me now," Logan whispered. "Why not?" asked McCormick in surprise. "Because I might lose my job," said Logan. McCormick kept quiet and Logan kept his job, but of the two shows only *Stags at Bay* was a success.

As happens to most theater people sooner or later, Logan received an unexpected summons from Hollywood in the spring of 1936—to direct dialogue for *Garden of Allah*, starring Charles Boyer and Marlene Dietrich. His first day in the picture business was not auspicious. Excited by the prospect of a reunion with Fonda and Stewart, who were then sharing a house in Hollywood and had invited him to be their guest, Logan did not sleep during his flight to the Coast or open the novel *Garden of Allah*, which he had planned to study en route. On landing he was whisked directly to a story conference at the Selznick studio, where he seemed so vague and devoid of ideas about *Garden of Allah* that David O. Selznick finally snapped in exasperation: "Speak up, Logan. We brought you all the way out here and we want to hear some opinions!" Logan somehow double-talked his way through the conference, which lasted until dawn the next morning. When it was over, Selznick offered him a lift in his car. As the chauffeur drove through a gate between bronze lions and up a driveway bordered with meticulous palms and shrubbery, Logan's sleepy eyes bulged. "Boy, is Fonda putting on the dog!" he sneered. "Now I know what going Hollywood means. This is just plain bad taste." From beside him Selznick said quietly, "This is my house." Despite this beginning, Logan's Hollywood sojourn turned out well. Both Boyer and Dietrich liked his work—so much indeed that Boyer asked him to direct his next picture, *History Is Made at Night*. Logan stayed on the Coast long enough to make a third film, *I Met My Love Again*, which he helped write as well as direct.

Shortly after Logan returned to Broadway, financially invigorated by his movie work, Producer Dwight Wiman invited him to direct Paul Osborne's fine play, *On Borrowed Time*.

"I couldn't believe it had been offered to me," he later told a friend. "For years I had seen nothing but plays that had fallen through the sieve of the big directors—only the thinnest, most watery substance." He and Osborne agreed the last few scenes were not right, and for four months they worked together, writing and rewriting the final twenty minutes of the play. The morning after the opening, Critic Brooks Atkinson wrote in the New York *Times*: "Something blissful has come to town." *On Borrowed Time* was not only Logan's first hit, it is still remembered as an enduring model of luminous and restrained directorial art. Logan followed up this success with three hearty musicals: *I Married an Angel, Knickerbocker Holiday,* and *Stars in Your Eyes,* all hits. Thus by the age of thirty he had established himself as A Very Fine Director and was even described by some as A Genius, though musicals do not usually count toward being A Genius.

It was at this point, when royalties and offers were cascading in and it seemed as though his prime ambitions had been fulfilled, that a complex chain of circumstances began to evolve which were to lead him barely a year later into a mental institution. Drained by his labors, Logan agreed to go on a trip with a friend from the University Players, John Swope, who had abandoned the stage for photography and was on his way to South America to take pictures. For eight months he and Swope ranged the South American continent, penetrating the wildest areas and finally crossing the Straits to Tierra del Fuego and Cape Horn. Near the end of the trip, in a moment of vanity and "fat-hypochondria" (Logan's term for his chronic worry about weight) he decided to reduce. For days he had nothing but orange juice. His weight fell from 195 to 175. And then it kept on falling.

It continued to fall after he had returned to New York and started work on another play by Paul Osborne, *Morning's at Seven*. By then he was down to 165 and very weak. Logan lasted through just six days of rehearsals. On the seventh day he collapsed and was taken to a hospital, where he spent the next month desperately ill with nausea and fevers ranging up to 105. *Morning's at Seven* opened to tepid notices and closed after six weeks (though it was subsequently included in the *Ten Best Plays of 1939–40*). When Logan emerged from the hospital, still weak and morbidly disappointed by what he took to be his own failure, he was driven by a frenzy to redeem himself immediately and he again made the error of taking two jobs at the same time. In the mornings he directed sketches for a revue called *Two for the Show;* afternoons and evenings he collaborated on the book of a musical comedy called *Higher and Higher*. He became more and more despondent, dissatisfied with his work, and critical of himself. For the first time in his life the future seemed empty of hope. "Had anyone convinced me then I was in a state of abnormal depression and ought to see a psychiatrist," he observed afterward, "I would gladly have gone. But everyone just said 'Pull yourself together. Snap out of it.' " Ultimately *Higher and Higher* played to good houses, but the critics condemned it and the notices rankled inordinately. At another time Logan, for all his thin skin, might have viewed this chapter as a vicissitude of the theater. Instead he decided he had betrayed his artistic standards and he felt humiliated and debased.

At this ebb point Logan impulsively embarked on a brief and ill-starred marriage which lasted but a few unhappy weeks and then dissolved. His mind thereupon took one of those mysterious protective measures which psychology only partly understands. Subtly, without realizing it himself, he swung out of his depression into an opposite phase; he entered what psychiatrists call a state of manic elation, a condition of great vigor and self-assurance in which no problem seemed too difficult and no task too great. In this mood of high optimism he undertook to direct a revival of the ancient farce, *Charley's Aunt,* though most of his associates considered it a dubious project and his own agent advised against it. Today critics remember the première of *Charley's Aunt* as a kind of dopester's upset analogous in its way to the elections of 1948. "Most of us approached the opening of that revival with grave misgivings," John Mason Brown wrote afterward. "But we were wrong—happily and completely wrong. We had not foreseen Mr. Ferrer's superb abilities as a farceur or the sheer wizardry of Mr. Logan's direction." What Logan achieved was the transmutation of a museum piece into a fresh and hilarious comedy; he made the audience laugh *with* it rather than *at* it. Never before had his direction been so fluid and inventive. He infused the production with a vitality and enthusiasm that literally held the company together; some of the actors had been deeply pessimistic, and Nedda Harrigan, playing the title role, tried to withdraw from the company three times. Never before had Logan worked so hard. Night after night he never slept at all.

Afterward he slept even less, and gradually his friends came to realize his energies were abnormal. Riding the crest of his notices, he made deals in all directions, agreeing to direct this play and that movie, and to put money into dozens of doubtful ventures. He was engulfed in scripts and enchained by his telephone. After dark he prowled the night clubs restlessly, talking to anyone who would listen, telling stories to cabdrivers, show girls, waiters, just to hear them laugh. When he went home he read until dawn; he found he could absorb the contents of a whole page or memorize a poem at a glance; his mind had never seemed so clear. And he never slept.

At length his mother induced him to consult a psychiatrist, who told him he had suffered a severe nervous breakdown and advised him to enter a hospital at once. Fearful and haunted by all he had to do, Logan refused. Only after two more doctors had reiterated the urgency of his condition did he submit to hospitalization—but with the stipulation that no doors should be locked and no strong drugs administered. For a month he fretted in voluntary confinement, reading scores of books, writing poetry, and studying French and Spanish grammar. Suspicious of his attendants, he dropped letters out his window, hoping passers-by would post them. When friends sent him flowers he sent them back or tossed them to children playing in the street below. Once on finding his door locked he climbed onto a narrow ledge outside his window and perched there until the door was opened. He finally talked his doctors into letting him move to a friend's house in the country, but despite the change and outdoor exercise he still could not sleep. After a while he slipped away to New York, where he wandered at large for several nights, seeing plays. Then he disappeared.

A few days later the producers of an unpretentious musical show rehearsing in Boston were agreeably surprised by an unexpected visit from Logan, who offered to put ten thousand dollars into their production provided he could make some changes. They agreed and he went to work at once, rewriting and restaging with extraordinary insight and vigor. Word of his presence got back to New York, however, and one day a

Boston psychiatrist named Merrill Moore wandered into the theater and introduced himself. Taking an immediate liking to him, Logan agreed to pay him daily visits. Dr. Moore explained the nature of his illness and advised him to exploit his elation while it lasted—to attempt things he had always wanted to do and could master now more easily than ever again. Under Dr. Moore's deft guidance Logan withdrew from the show and returned to his French and Spanish lessons; he taught himself to play the piano and to paint; he went to the Y.M.C.A. and found he could walk on his hands and do acrobatic dives. But he still could not sleep, and just before Christmas Dr. Moore went away to a convention in Philadelphia.

At once the theater drew Logan like a magnet. He went down to New York and invited the entire company of *Charley's Aunt* to a party. He bought presents for everyone, ordered cases of Chablis and sparkling Burgundy, trimmed a huge Christmas tree, and then sat down amid the glitter to await his guests. Of all he had invited only two showed up—one was Nedda Harrigan. Yet the party was big and noisy, for Logan called in bellhops, chambermaids, and anyone who happened by and gave them presents and wine until everything was gone. Next day on an impulse he set out for Princeton; but he felt frightened, dizzy, and exhausted, so he went on to Philadelphia to look for Dr. Moore. The streets bewildered him and the faces of the passers-by seemed strangely vivid. A couplet by Emily Dickinson chattered in his head: "I'm nobody! Who are you? Are you nobody, too?" Late that night he found Dr. Moore in his hotel. "What can I do? What can I do?" he asked despairingly. "Josh," Dr. Moore said gravely, "you've got to go to a hospital." "Why?" Logan asked. "Because you might die," the doctor said. Pains suddenly tore through Logan's body and he fancied that death was at hand. "You've got to go of your own accord," the doctor continued, "you must commit yourself." But Logan stubbornly said, "I can't go. I've got so many things to do, I've made so many promises." Dr. Moore looked at him quietly and said, "Listen to me carefully," and then quoted an entire poem by Robert Frost. The last lines were:

> The woods are lovely, dark and deep.
> But I have promises to keep,
> And miles to go before I sleep,
> And miles to go before I sleep.

The aptness and aesthetic appeal of the lines melted Logan's defenses and he went to his room promising to commit himself in the morning. But once alone his fears swept over him again. He decided he would run away from himself; he would change his identity. He trampled on his clothes and rubbed dirt on his face. Then he crept downstairs and began wandering through the streets. Hours later he hailed a cab and collapsed in the back seat. "Take me to Pennsylvania Hospital," he said.

For a moment when he read the sign on the gate, "For Mental and Nervous Diseases," he recoiled. But something impelled him to pass through, and once inside he signed a paper committing himself until the hospital agreed to let him go. At once a wave of tranquillity enveloped him and he fell asleep. Logan remained in the hospital for three months, during which he played baseball and golf, swam, studied Spanish and sculpture; he wrote poems, stories, and plays; he composed music, painted, built a model theater, and set type. One day a pall of despondency lowered on him; he saw his whole experience in retrospect and was appalled by it. "Now," the doctors told him, "you're getting well."

When he left the hospital Logan was warned to stay away from the theater for six months. In this transition period he and his sister Mary Lee, whose husband had died a little over two years after their marriage, went to Boston and took courses at Harvard in philosophy, Italian art, and music. On New Year's Day, 1942, Dr. Moore told Logan he could go back to work. He was immediately engaged to direct Richard Rodgers's musical *By Jupiter*. Logan feared that actors would not trust him any more, but Dr. Moore reassured him: "They'll just look at you and they'll know you're all right." Although he took the job with misgivings, it was evident at once that his talents had matured in exile and *By Jupiter* proved a notable hit.

When a friend asked him not long ago to define the terms of his utmost ambition, Logan replied thoughtfully: "I would like to find a way of living that is not so turbulent and full of pressure, and involves no responsibility for other people's lives. I would like to stay in a small Italian village and write violent stories about a kind of life I do not lead. I would like to do nonsense things with my wife, to plant gardens we never see. I would like to be lazy. All my life I've really been lazy and have pushed myself because of the exhilaration of the theater. I think most of all I'd like to be a bum, a dirty lousy bum who smells bad and never bathes and never wears a tie and goes through life with the smallest amount of muscular and mental effort possible—a nasty, lazy, worthless, no-good bastard. That dream recurs and recurs."

Anyone who knows Logan would realize that this is a lot of dramatic hokum. The day he gives up the theater will be the day he gives up respiration.

The Silent Tears
By Claudia McNeil

Claudia McNeil shot to stardom in the Broadway play, Raisin
in the Sun, *and also appeared in the movie. In 1966, she won
the London Theatre Critics Award as the best actress of the
year, for her performance in* The Amen Corner. *She also appeared on Broadway in the comedy,* Something Different,
written by Carl Reiner.

I went into analysis to discover the answers to two questions.
I was unable to cry at the death of my two sons in Korea, and
I wanted to know why I could not cry.

And, a very prominent man who was not Negro wanted to
marry me and I wouldn't marry him. I thought it might be because I was frightened of the outcome. He was a rich man, a
noted writer, and he tried to convince me that our marriage

would not affect him. But I couldn't see it that way, I was too scared of miscegenation. I adore my Negro race and wanted to be attractive to all men but mainly to Negro men. And I wanted to know whether I was right in thinking this.

About this time I met Ann Cutler, a writer in the medical field, and talked to her about my problems. She said, "Claudia, why don't you go to one of these men?" She was writing a book on psychiatry and she gave me the names of two psychiatrists.

"What do I need a headshrinker for?" I demanded.

"Are you afraid of psychiatry?" she asked.

"I'm so disciplined and stabilized I can figure things out for myself," I said.

"I think you should go to a psychiatrist," Ann insisted. "I can't help you any more than by telling you this."

It was 1959. I went to the first name she suggested. I liked him right off, although he seemed a little stoic. I thought, "I'll kick this around for a bit."

Then I found that every Friday morning at eleven, I looked forward to seeing him. Even though he wouldn't resolve anything for me.

"You haven't given me any solution to what's bothering me," I would say.

"No. You're not to depend on me. You're to stand on your own two feet," he would answer.

Lord, he would irritate me with that remark. I would say angrily (I don't playact in real life, I leave my role in the theater), "I'm going to get up and throw a book right at your head. You make me so mad!"

"If you feel that way, Claudia, go ahead and throw it." He would hand me a book.

Of course I wouldn't throw it. Then he would say, "You're so perceptive, it's not even funny. You have exceptional clarity in your thought except when it comes to a man you're in love with. Then you have no clarity."

"So tell me what to do," I would beg.

"No," and he would shake his head.

Then I would threaten, "I can't throw a book but I'm going to slam that door so hard the knob will come off when I leave."

"If it pleases you, Claudia, slam the door," he would say.

But I could never slam the door either.

Sometimes he would put me under hypnosis. I would concentrate on the brass lamp. I was finally able to cry, under the hypnosis. I would come out of it ashamed of the tears streaming down my face. My mother was an Apache Indian and we were taught that crying was a sign of weakness.

But the analyst taught me to cry. He taught me that crying was *not* a sign of weakness. I cried eight times a week on the stage of *Raisin*. I used to hum, "Nearer My God to Thee" or think of some tragedy. But, as I said, I could not shed a tear when I lost my two sons, one twenty, the other, twenty-one.

They were always very close. Where one went, the other went, too. I raised them with freedom and abandon, but always with respect for authority, most of all respect for themselves. I taught them never to let anyone take away from them a personal sense of their own worth. If you have your own sense of worth, nobody can destroy you.

One day they came to me and said, "Look here, old gal, we want you to enjoy yourself. If we stay with you, you won't go out and find a husband. You've had no luck with your guys so far, since we've been with you. So maybe our going will change that." One of them said, I forget which one, "You're a sexpot and somebody ought to get the advantage of it."

I had to let them go. You have to let children go at the right time.

They loved the Air Force. They told me, "We think we live in the greatest country in the world and we want to give it back some of what we get from it. We can do that by fighting."

When I was informed by the Air Force that they had both been killed, I just couldn't cry. Instead, I dropped things all over the place—ashtrays, dishes, articles off the bureau. Instead of dropping tears, I guess I was dropping things.

My analysis was one of the happiest experiences of my life. Actually, it resolved my life for me. I saw the analyst for two years, until 1961. Then a national tour with "Raisin" interrupted analysis. When I returned home, which is New York, the city in which I grew up, I saw the analyst again for a few months.

My problem with the Caucasian writer was solved when he married a prominent Hollywood actress. Meanwhile two friends (with friends like this, you don't need enemies) introduced me to a man who, if he was cast as an actor, would be a banker or lawyer. I married him, and I never paid so much for so little in all my life.

It was so disastrous a marriage that I had to find out why I went into it. I hate loose ends. This was 1964 and I saw the analyst once again for several months after my divorce.

I told him that I wanted to know why, after waiting so long to get married the second time, I had picked the wrong man. When I have trouble resolving something, I know it's me. I have to figure out why I'm in that trouble.

The analyst helped me realize that I deserved what I got. I had married not out of love but because I wanted to marry a Negro man, to avoid any inter-racial conflict, and also because I felt that Negro men rejected me, wanting light-skinned girls, size 12. I had married the first colored man who proposed, look ing for an escape hatch.

My first marriage took place when we both were youngsters. He was the first man I ever kissed. We married to keep from running away from our homes. He was a wonderful man but we didn't know what we were doing. The marriage broke up after the second baby, and we were divorced in 1946. It wasn't until 1962 that I married again. Meanwhile I kept getting engaged and breaking engagements. The analyst said my standards for men were too high.

"But what'll I talk to them about?" I asked. "I want an intelligent man."

The analyst said, "Claudia, you have to learn the art of compromise. You're not going to find the kind of man you're looking for. He went out with the Saxons. You have a story-book version of the modern man. He just doesn't exist."

Life is a series of chains, each experience linked to the next. For instance, in the analysis we talked about how ugly I had always felt. My mother told me every day of my life, during the twelve years I lived with her, that I was the ugliest woman in the world because I looked like my father, not her.

"The only thing you can do is work hard and be a domestic, Claudia," she would say.

It was doubly hard because my older sister was beautiful. And I always had the feeling that, no matter what I did, I would be ugly. Friends would urge me to put on makeup, look pretty.

"What's the point? It's not going to do any good," I would say.

Sometimes they would get furious and yell at me, "Claudia, it's time you stopped that!"

It was Walter Kerr who put the cap on the bottle. One time Jean Kerr asked why I sent her a beautiful bouquet when she was having a baby. Nobody ever sends a baby anything, just the mother, and I thought of designing two nosegays, one small, one large, attached to each other with a ribbon, like an umbilical cord. I had a florist make it up and took it to the hospital. Sometime later, one night in Sardi's, when Jean was pregnant with another baby, she asked me why I had sent the bouquet.

I told her that something Walter had written had changed my life. Even with analysis, and my own Catholicism, which I believe in fervently and couldn't do without, I still could not change my feelings about myself. But Walter wrote about me, in 1962, when I appeared in "Tiger, Tiger, Burning Bright," that "Claudia has the face of a Buddha."

After that, in spite of the fact that my marriage was breaking up, and I was having trouble with the director, who was having troubles of his own, I felt very happy. From that day to this, I have never had the feeling that I was ugly. My mother's voice, telling me so, has melted away, and so has all my anger at her.

After Walter's review, I went right out and bought a sleeveless chiffon aquamarine evening gown that dragged the floor, because I felt so good. I had always been a skinny child but put on weight in later years and was ashamed of my plump arms. To please the analyst, I would go and stand in front of Lane Bryant and realize that other women had plump arms, too. But it didn't seem to help.

Actually, what Walter said would not have affected me so deeply if I hadn't been working on it in analysis. But I didn't believe the analyst. I did believe Walter. He was another link in the chain.

During the analysis, we talked about my childhood. When I was twelve, I went to the Hecksher Foundation, which had a plan to help children, and said I wanted to leave home. My mother appeared before the officials and frankly told them, "My daughter has the ways of the Apache but she doesn't look like the Apache. She would never be mean or vicious but she has the indifference of the Apache, and that I can't stand. She can wipe you off the face of the earth with that indifference."

I went to work as a Mother's Helper. If you weren't delinquent or had not been touched by boys, they let you go out and sleep as a domestic. Then I was adopted by a Jewish couple. They told me they needed me, a beautiful way to tell a child you want to adopt him. Everyone needs to be needed. They asked me if I wanted to join the family, they had two other children, and, of course, I did.

We spent hours talking about my childhood in the analysis, and I saw how some experiences had contributed to the conflicts I had, but how many had given me the strength I needed to become an actress.

I feel today that I don't want to marry again. I certainly would *never* marry an actor. Then who'd get custody of the mirror?

I love actors. I adore them. But I would not marry one. I know too many actors who think they can hug a scrapbook or talk to a bankbook.

I feel contented. I love people. I'm at peace with myself. I love books; I used to work in a library. I go to the theater, when I'm in a play, two hours early, sometimes to read, sometimes just to sit and talk to the wardrobe mistress or a prop man. I love television. I wouldn't miss my favorite shows.

One of the biggest disappointments of my life was when Adlai Stevenson was not elected President. The country didn't want a man with humor. The only way the Negro can exist is to laugh. With laughter, he can live with his brown skin, in this divided world of ours.

Despite the sympathy and understanding many Caucasians have for the problems of the Negro, no amount of imagination can possibly allow them to fully understand what it is like to have a brown skin.

That is why the Negro has to laugh so much. Although I've always had humor, analysis heightened my sense of humor, and for that, too, I am grateful.

I Didn't Grow Up To Be President
By Dr. Harold Greenwald

Dr. Greenwald is author of several books, including Great Cases in Psychoanalysis, The Call Girl, *a social and psychoanalytic study,* Emotional Maturity in Love and Marriage *with Lucy Freeman, and most recently,* Active Psychotherapy. *In addition, he is president of the National Psychological Association for Psychoanalysis.*

The Institute had given me three or four names of analysts to choose for my training analysis. It had been difficult to accept the fact that I needed therapy so I went about it in a roundabout way. I decided that I would become an analyst, knowing that as an analyst, I would need to be analyzed.

That wasn't my only reason. Ever since the eighth grade I had been reading books about psychoanalysis, had been fascinated by it, but had never gotten around to doing anything more concrete. One day as I was reading a book by Theodor Reik, I realized that he was not a physician and yet he was a world renowned psychoanalyst. Impulsively, I wrote him a letter asking him where a nonmedical person could get training. By return mail and in his own handwriting, he answered that letter. (Since then I have taken it as my duty also to answer letters from people who have read any of my books and who have written to me.)

Dr. Reik's answer was to cause a most profound change in my life. He wrote me about the National Psychological Association for Psychoanalysis then just starting its training institute. I entered the first class at the Association, where I was told that in order to complete my work at the Institute, I would need a personal analysis.

It is strange what a capacity for self-deception we all have. When I went to my analyst the first day, one I had chosen only because he was more conveniently located near my home than any of the other people on my list, I remember feeling nervous but I didn't feel the nervousness as anxiety, I experienced it rather as excitement. So I was excited when I rang his bell and he opened the door and let me into his simple, comfortable office.

I sat down and he looked up at me and asked in words that have since become very familiar through my own use of them, "How can I help you?"

I said I would like to be analyzed and he asked, "For what reason?"

I replied, "I want to become an analyst and in order to be one, I know I have to be analyzed."

"Well, what problems do you have?" he asked.

"No special problems. I want to be an analyst and so I want to be analyzed."

He looked at me seriously and said, "If you have no problems, I can't help you."

That is what I meant when I spoke about my capacity for self-deception.

I was in my late thirties and, to all extents and purposes, a failure. Not that I wasn't earning some sort of living; I was working at a job that I frequently hated and despised and this was the best job I had held up to that date, or maybe the second best. In this job I found myself surrounded by people with whom I had nothing in common, doing work which, with rare exception, had very little meaning for me. I was using a small fraction of my ability; as far as work satisfaction was concerned, I had been a prime example of occupational maladjustment. In the seventeen years that I had been out of college, I had held sixty different jobs that had included among other things, teaching, social work, technical writing, fund raising, industrial engineering, press agent, management consultant, reporter, and personnel director. But I had not done the kind of work that I found fulfilling. The fact that I had changed jobs so frequently indicated how unsatisfactory an occupational adjustment I had made.

While I loved my wife and children (the youngest had just been born), the bitterness which I experienced about my work, the self-hate I frequently faced when occupied with some idiotic task in which I had little interest, so poisoned my feelings that it was difficult to be the kind of father and husband I would have liked to have been.

Yet when I sat in front of my analyst on that first memorable day I said that I didn't know what problems I had, that I just wanted to be analyzed because I needed it. Until that point, I felt I would never be able to complete any additional education. I had managed to finish high school and college with a minimum of work: not because I was disinterested but because I found it impossible to discipline myself to do the required studying. If I had just listened in class instead of daydreaming, I might have been able to do quite well. Instead, I just slid through. Therefore, I was certain that I would never be capable of handling the hard work required to get through medical school. I was not aware that with my retentive ability, it would have been much less work for me than for most people. Still, I had been too fearful of what I now know was my self-destructive attitude to even think of going to medical school. It was for that reason that Dr. Reik's letter had been such a godsend.

Most of my analysis focused on this work problem. I also began to understand more about my relationship with my family—my rivalries, angers and disappointments. But basically, the major focus was on work.

As a result of my analysis, I not only completed my work at the Institute, but after finishing, decided to go to Columbia University to get a doctorate in psychology. Instead of slipping through as I had as an undergraduate, I managed to complete the work in the entire course and the writing of the dissertation in three years. Not only did I complete it in this comparatively short time while working full-time and supporting my family, but my dissertation was later adapted into a book *The Call Girl*, which sold approximately 1,000,000 copies. It was also translated into several foreign languages including Japanese, and was eventually made into a motion picture. A far cry from the young man who had been incapable of carrying through the simple tasks which I had been assigned in my various jobs.

What made the change? What were the problems? It is hard to see all of them, even at this late date. However, some is clear.

First, was the fact that I had received rewards before I ever had to earn them. At age four, I was known in the family as the "little genius." What need was there for me to struggle or to do anything, if I was already bestowed the title of "genius?" When I entered school, things went not at all smoothly. Instead of recognizing my genius the teachers were extremely critical of my restlessness and misconduct. I felt this was because I was bored. School *was* slow and dull. After the first grade, I read most of my textbooks during the first week. It was painfully boring for me to sit in class. At that time the procedure of skipping a grade was quite common, but since I had become a conduct problem and was generally involved in some kind of mischief, such as talking, my grades were generally poor. They did not reflect my work ability but my "conduct," as it was then termed. The only time I managed to skip was in the seventh grade when I was in a class only seven days due to the many holidays that occurred in September. I hadn't yet managed to get into enough trouble, so I was skipped on the basis of class work, rather than deportment. It was only after I was skipped and challenged with more difficult work that I was able to do well all term.

I had been given great praise as a young child by my parents, but I had turned out to be a terrible disappointment. I remember the day that I graduated from elementary school. My mother attended and because I received no awards she became hysterical when she came home. I also remember a neighbor putting wet towels on her head and saying, "Don't worry, maybe you'll have some pleasure from your other sons." Obviously, I had been given up as a lost cause.

If I analyze the reason for the change, I think I would have to put it in other terms. My major problem was that I made enormous demands on myself. Normal functioning was not good enough. I had gone through school, I *did* go through high school, and I did go through City College. But *that* wasn't enough. The demands, the unreal expectations that had been placed upon me by my mother, particularly, and which I had internalized, made it impossible for me to really function effectively. One scene stands out in my mind because I believe it was oft repeated—coming home from kindergarten at twelve o'clock, for lunch with my mother. I would ask, "What will happen to me, what will be my future?"

My mother would answer, "You'll become president of a college and then you will become a governor and then President of the United States." She was of course echoing the life plan of Woodrow Wilson who had recently been elected President. Anything short of becoming President of the United States would thus be seen as a failure. As I grew older, I became aware of the difficulty of obtaining that job. And since my subsequent work at school didn't show much promise of a future as President, I made unreal demands on myself that I couldn't possibly fulfill. I was, therefore, paralyzed.

To this day I often wonder what happened in analysis that caused me to modify these self-demands. What happened that made it possible for me to accept a more realistic set of goals and therefore to accomplish much more than I had in the close to forty years before analysis?

One thing was perhaps serendipitous, that is, it was a result of luck, or unsought for, or perhaps unpremeditated by my analyst. When I went to take the examination that would qualify me for the doctoral program, I remember telling him that it wasn't going to be a problem because I always did well in such exams. I really was sort of boasting. He indicated that it wasn't necessary to do all that well, and I think, also questioned whether I would. It happened that I did extremely well and therefore was admitted into a program in which very few of the many applicants were accepted. As a result of that incident our relationship grew. For one thing, my analyst never made unreal demands on me; he didn't give me unreal goals.

He seemed to be interested in other things than the goal of great achievement. I didn't have to become President of the United States to satisfy him. All he seemed to want was for me to examine and experience my feelings. It took me a long time, it is true, to recognize how important this is, and to admit, easily and naturally, to my many shortcomings and difficulties. When I found that I could admit them and still retain his respect and general good will, I think this, combined with the lack of pressure, helped to create the change. The major achievement of my first analysis was the ability to drop some of my unreal goals.

When I returned to school, to graduate school that is, I no longer considered it beneath me to study for an exam. I no longer considered it beneath me to prepare a paper carefully. Previously, my notions about myself and my demands on myself had been so inflated that I would have considered it an act of humiliation to study for an examination. My long battle with authority had to some small extent been resolved.

Several years after I finished individual analysis, was working with patients, and had written a book, I decided, chiefly because I was interested in the technique of the particular analyst, to enter group therapy. This was a completely different experience for me. I was able to feel the hatred and anger and fury that I had long ago repressed. In my first analysis I had learned about things intellectually, or had been able to look back at experiences. In the group, the situation was different. It wasn't that I remembered an experience, it wasn't that I understood it, but that I actually experienced some of the intense rage and hate and despair that I had gone through as a very young child.

If the individual analysis had made me more successful and given me the capacity for work at one level, the group experience enabled me to experience anger, hate, love, warmth—much more than I ever had in my life. It made me understand others. It was of enormous assistance in my work, both in individual and group therapy.

This brings me to a problem that I have wrestled with for a long time. With many of my patients, after the immediate problems are disposed of and the symptoms have cleared up, something else becomes apparent. Frequently, I realize that the symptoms and difficulties mask something very different, something much more fundamental, which patients describe in different ways. Some speak of it as the "void"; some speak of it as the feeling of emptiness; some call it a general dissatisfaction with life, or describe it in terms of neurotic, self-destructive, desperate attitudes (bringing to mind what Thoreau said: "Most men lead lives of quiet desperation.") All this appears to refer to the same kind of phenomenon—the feeling of emptiness, the feeling of what is now a popular term, "alienation." This is the problem to which we often have to dedicate ourselves and one which is extremely difficult to deal with.

I think much of the literature of our century, certainly the vogue for existentialism and for existential analysis, tries to solve this problem.

When this problem becomes salient in my work with a patient, it is difficult to know at all times what to do. With some, I urge its acceptance as a human condition which we all must face. But often a patient turns to me and says, "You don't have this problem." And I must admit that I experience it less than most people I know. One patient, a very bright perceptive young lady, was constantly torturing herself and her husband because fundamentally she worried about this feeling of emptiness, of uselessness, or purposelessness.

"How did *you* get away from it?" she asks. "What makes *you* so smart?"

Then I realized that the reason I suffer so little from this problem is that I never completely resolved the problem of making extraordinary demands on myself. It is true that I modified these demands, modified them drastically, but in the words of Browning, "Oh, that a man's reach should exceed his grasp, else what's a heaven for." It is because my ambitions, my goals, are just beyond anything that I can ever accomplish, that I keep going, that I find life a constant challenge and excitement.

For example, at the moment I have four books outlined which I would like to write. At the same time, I have a full schedule of patients. There are three different institutes at which I teach, in addition to acting as consultant to an agency. I also constantly accept speaking assignments and am even willing to speak on radio and television programs. All of these activities keep me so busy, so stimulated with the new challenge that each activity represents, that it is difficult for me to experience the void that many persons describe. But at the same time I know that I have to be careful not to make the demands on myself too excessive, or I won't be able to do anything. An amusing example is the fact that, for years, I wasn't able to start any book because I really wanted to do four at the same time. Fortunately, I have decided not to write the great definitive book on psychology but to satisfy myself with writing books as well as I can on subjects which are less demanding than the large overall topic I would like to challenge.

Of course, as an analyst, I have a great advantage. I am constantly faced by individuals with problems similar to mine, with backgrounds that are similar in certain respects, and I've had the opportunity of observing how they handle their lives. Often, in becoming involved in working with them, in helping them solve their problems, I help myself as well. I've also been fortunate in that many of my patients would rather spend time helping me, than concentrating on themselves, and so reward me for my attention by telling me what is wrong with me and how I can improve. Thus, I had not only an individual analyst, a group analyst, and four splendid supervisors or control analysts, but by now, hundreds of patient-analysts who know me only too well.